The Babinski Reflex

The Babinski Reflex

And 70 Other
Useful and Amusing Metaphors
from
Science, Psychology, Business,
Sports,
and Everyday Life

Philip Goldberg

JEREMY P. TARCHER, INC.
Los Angeles

Library of Congress Cataloging-in-Publication Data

Goldberg, Philip, 1944–
  The Babinski reflex, and 70 other useful and amusing metaphors from
science, psychology, business, sports, and everyday life / by Philip Goldberg.
      p.   cm.
  ISBN 0-87477-563-9
    1. English language—Terms and phrases.   2. Metaphor.   I. Title.
PE1689.G65   1990   89-20689
423'.1—dc20   CIP

Jeremy P. Tarcher, Inc.
5858 Wilshire Blvd., Suite 200
Los Angeles, CA 90036

Distributed by St. Martin's Press, New York

Design by Robert Tinnon
Illustrations by Giora Carmi

Manufactured in the United States of America
10 9 8 7 6 5 4 3 2 1

First Edition

To my wife, Jane,
who loves words and ideas
as well as the author.

Contents

❦

Preface

The greatest thing in style is to have command of
  metaphor.
                                —Aristotle: Poetics XXII

One thing that literature would be
  greatly the better for
Would be a more restricted employment
  by authors of simile and metaphor.
                                —Ogden Nash

This book is for people who feel
more like Aristotle than Ogden Nash. Lovers of language know
that a well-placed metaphor, like great drama, simultaneously
enriches and enlightens. Suitably rendered and properly placed,
a metaphor can provide the surprise of a magic trick or a
punch line, the esthetic kick of a well-placed chord, the illuminating jolt of a solved puzzle. The unexpected liaison of
two seemingly incongruous entities grabs the attention and
excites the emotions, thereby making a metaphoric statement
more memorable than a prosaic rendering of the same idea.

Our brains appear to be wired for metaphor. From childhood on, we make life comprehensible by using comparisons
when straightforward explication fails. Not only wordsmiths,
but painters and composers use metaphoric forms to elevate
their art. Mathematicians create metaphors of symbols. Inven-

tors forge metaphorical links between man-made gadgets and the apparatus of nature. Politicians and rhetoricians use metaphors to persuade, agitate, inspire, and inflame. Scientists grope for metaphors when trying to make sense of their observations and grope again when attempting to make their abstractions concrete enough for the laity to comprehend. And in everyday discourse, we all attempt to enliven and clarify our speech with analogies ("My trip to city hall was straight out of Kafka"), similes ("He's as cold as ice"), and metaphors ("I'm in the autumn of my life").

This book approaches metaphoric thinking in its loosest sense—metaphor as figurative speech, a way to enrich or enlighten by stretching terminology beyond its conventional context. It was conceived over lunch with my publisher, Jeremy Tarcher, one of those rare entrepreneurs who manages to keep his enterprises growing while also keeping them small enough for the founders to do what they like best—in this case, dreaming up new ideas. Jeremy was interested in a compilation of concepts, principally from science, that warrant a place in the vocabulary of culturally literate people. He had in mind terms that an educated person should know, or may have already learned but had long since forgotten. The rationale was this: because our culture is fragmented into specialized disciplines that evolve their own esoteric jargons, those of us outside each specialty are by and large left unaware of insights and discoveries that can enrich our understanding of ourselves and our world. The book would help to fill that gap.

It was envisioned as a "fun-fact book," which would describe in nontechnical language the origins and salient themes of important concepts (along with some not-so-important ones that were just plain interesting). When it seemed that most of the terms Jeremy had in mind had the word *effect* in their names (the Butterfly Effect, the Greenhouse Effect, the Doppler Effect, etc.), it came to be called "The Effects Book." But it rapidly took on added dimensions.

Not only would "effects" alone not suffice—there are "principles," "laws," "theorems," "factors," "syndromes," and more— but we realized that the most fascinating of these ideas were those whose utility transcends their original intent. These may have originated in physics or politics or experimental psychology, but they were metaphorically fertile in that they reminded us of situations we all might find ourselves in—at work, at home, in love, in a supermarket. They were not just effects; they were *metaffects*.

The Greek root *meta* means "involving change." I combined *meta* with *effect* to denote the spirit of change or transference implied in such words as metamorphosis, metabolism, metallurgy, and, of course, metaphor. A metaffect, then, is a recognized effect, law, or principle whose official meaning can be transferred to another context. The Babinski Reflex, for example, is a term describing an automatic response in the foot of an infant, thought to be a vestige of our primate ancestry. As such, it resonates metaphorically (or *metaffectively*) with certain forms of adult behavior that might be considered primitive or infantile, such as erupting in a temper tantrum over some trivial offense. One can easily imagine the term catching on and being used either for a laugh or to drive home a point. That qualifies it as a metaffect.

In assembling terms to choose from, I scoured (with the noteworthy help of my wife) the indexes and glossaries of reference books, textbooks, and selected works of nonfiction; browsed through specialized dictionaries and encyclopedias; picked the brains of friends and acquaintances; and posted solicitations on computer bulletin boards. Along the way, the search expanded beyond academic and scientific disciplines and entered arenas such as mountain climbing (the Fiddle Factor), military history (Fabian Tactics), politics (the Chappaquidick Theorem), and educational testing (the Lake Wobegon Effect). I accumulated a few hundred terms in all, from which I eventually selected the final entries based on three criteria.

First, the term itself had to be of unusual interest, either because of its intrinsic fascination, its topicality, its origin, or its importance in intellectual history. Second, it had to be metaphorically rich, both in a practical sense and as entertainment; I leaned toward terms whose use would be fun and could easily be turned into a snappy quip or repartee. Third, it had to have a nice ring to it, so that it might stand out for its sound alone. (Babinski Reflex and Fosbury Flop are metaffects with particularly catchy names.)

Once the candidates had been selected, the final mix was chosen mainly with diversity in mind. The collection includes items from physics, chemistry, economics, philosophy, mathematics, sociology, medicine, astronomy; many from psychology and psychiatry; and some from such nonacademic areas as business, theater, law, and sports. About half are *eponyms*, terms named for a person—usually the person who discovered the principle (as with Bell's Theorem or Boyle's Law) but sometimes a mythological or literary figure (the Pygmalion Effect, the Jonah Complex, the Werther Effect)—or a person whose actions led others to name a principle after him or her (the Wallenda Factor). Among the noneponyms are terms named for metaphoric reasons (the Halo Effect, the Boomerang Effect) and others whose names are simply descriptive (the False Consensus Effect).

Among the entries are well-established principles known to everyone in the fields from which they derive; some, such as Gödel's Incompleteness Theorem and Heisenberg's Uncertainty Principle, are of central importance in the history of Western thought. Others are known to only a handful of people at this time and are of central importance to even fewer. Some metaffects are venerable; others are of relatively recent vintage. Most items have serious origins; others were coined for whimsical reasons or solely to make a clever point. I included terms that will never make a must-know list for the culturally literate simply because they were so provocative, humorous, or rich with metaffective potential that they fit the eclectic mixture nicely. Perhaps this showcase will elevate the more obscure terms to a higher level of prominence in the language.

Not included in the book are terms that have already become well-known metaffects. Culture Shock, Draconian Laws, the Law of Diminishing Returns, Parkinson's Law, the Peter Principle, Murphy's Law, the Domino Effect, the Ripple Effect, the Self-Fulfilling Prophecy, the Richter Scale, and others were originally coined to describe a specific principle or phenomenon but have since acquired the wider, metaphorical usage that the terms in the present collection might one day achieve. They are worth noting here not just for their absence, but as examples of how the language naturally incorporates such metaffects.

You should find that the terms in this book add flavor and punch to your vocabulary. As with all knowledge, knowing the names of salient concepts can be empowering. They represent wisdom from the universe and as such they can add insight and a certain measure of predictive control to everyday experience.

Using the metaffects will also influence your awareness in interesting ways. I found, as the terms crept into my consciousness, that I would notice examples of them in everyday events. Now I had a label for phenomena I had previously encountered, and this somehow enriched those experiences and helped put them in perspective, much the way that taking a course in astronomy adds a dimension to star-gazing or reading a book on jazz enhances one's appreciation of a performance. There is something about seeing a known principle from an arcane discipline manifested in the everyday world that exhilarates. It lends a touch of concrete reality to an abstract idea and an added layer of substance to the experience itself, enhancing one's perception of it.

In fact, there is a metaffect for this phenomenon: the Whorfian Hypothesis. Linguist Benjamin L. Whorf proposed that the nuances of each particular language actually shape the way speakers of the language perceive reality. Differences between languages, he said, don't merely reflect cultural differences, they *cause* cultural differences. Those who grow up speaking English, Whorf contended, think and perceive in a manner different from someone who grows up speaking Dutch or Mandarin or Swahili.

Although the Whorfian Hypothesis has been disputed by many scholars, it seems reasonable to assume that the structure of our language in some measure influences the way we perceive. That has certainly been my experience whenever I've added one of these metaffects to my vocabulary.

But there is another dimension to the use of metaffects in everyday speech—delight. The feeling reminds me of the joy in a child's face when he or she points at the correct object and exclaims, "Dog!" or "Chair!" or "Birdie!" Perhaps this is because a metaphoric (or metaffective) connection requires of the perceiver something more than mere observation; it takes a creative act of consciousness. Someone complains, for example, that his work is monotonous, so you tell him he needs the Coolidge Effect. Or because you're getting jostled around by an unruly mob in the subway, you think of Brownian Motion. The leap from office to sex research or from urban clamor to a petri dish is more than illuminating; it's a kick.

I suspect that this delight has metaphysical implications. Poets and mystics have always sung of the deep connections between the microcosm and the macrocosm and between the mind and the realm we call nature. Now scientists are speaking of interlacing threads that weave through the universe, discernible in the dance of galaxies and the buzz of electrons—and presumably in our own brains and by extension our thoughts, speech, and action. Perhaps, then, we are able to connect principles discovered by scientists and scholars with everyday events because the laws that run through and regulate the cosmos run through and regulate us. If that is so, then when we apply a metaffect, we put ourselves in touch, to some small degree, with something larger and more universal than ourselves. We remind ourselves that there is order in the universe, not random chaos—unity amid the crazy quilt diversity of existence. Perhaps the reward is a taste, a dew drop on the tongue of our souls, of the sense of unity that has moved those poets and mystics.

Insight, power, and sublime delight notwithstanding, I trust that at the very least you will have fun with the metaffects collected here. Fun was a welcome fringe benefit in researching the book, and providing the reader with the same was a chief goal in writing it. Have fun, then, and as they said in *Star Wars,* metaphors be with you.

And while you're at it, why not make up some metaffects of your own? Boyle may have had to slave over a hot test tube to discover his law and Doppler may have spent countless nights peering into the starry heavens to ascertain his effect, but you can apprehend principles, theorems, and syndromes in your office or home. With an observant eye and a critical mind, you might very well cognize the perfect name that captures why some people can't put the toothpaste cap back on the tube, why no one has ever been able to make stuffed cabbage like your mother, or why certain business associates can't consummate a deal without polluting it with rancor. Why shouldn't your name be affixed to the vocabulary like Parkinson's and Murphy's?

If you come up with a good metaffect, or uncover some good ones already named, please send them to me in care of the publisher for possible inclusion in a subsequent volume (see Afterword).

Acknowledgments

Much appreciation to Jeremy Tarcher for conceiving this project and entrusting it to me—and also for his ongoing enthusiasm and insightful suggestions regarding the content and structure of the book.

Thanks, too, to my editor, Rick Benzel, who shepherded the manuscript to completion. In addition to a sharp eye for errors and omissions, Rick contributed numerous ideas that enriched the book.

Many people suggested terms for inclusion in the book; they have my gratitude, as do the several experts who discussed concepts with me and helped to clarify their meanings. In addition to those whose names are mentioned in the text itself, I am particularly grateful to Michael Raleigh, Peter Conrad, Oscar Janiger, and Allyn Brodsky.

Finally, infinite thanks to my wife, Jane Brodie, who spent many hours combing reference books and typing entries into the computer. For her practical help with this book, but even more for her continuing support, compassion, and faith, I am deeply grateful.

The Achilles Syndrome

Achilles, great-grandson of Zeus, was a fearless, fierce, and relentless warrior. He also had a false sense of security. Despite a prophecy that said he would die at Troy, he led fifty Greek ships to the Trojan War and plunged headlong into battle.

If Achilles was cocky and indifferent to danger, it was with good reason: he thought he was invincible. His mother, Thetis the sea goddess, had dipped his infant body into the River Styx to make him immortal. Unfortunately, she had held her son by his heel during the plunge, keeping that single spot dry while the rest of the child's body was bathed by the potent waters of the Styx. The oversight proved to be fatal when Paris, Achilles' Trojan enemy, shot an arrow into his one area of vulnerability.

By rendering the story so majestically in "The Iliad," Homer did what Thetis could not: immortalize Achilles. As a result, we have the expression "Achilles' heel," which, of course, has come to signify a point of vulnerability.

Now psychiatrist and author Harold Bloomfield has taken the legend a step farther and given us an interesting metaffect: the *Achilles Syndrome*. This is, essentially, the tendency to deny our weak spots (Achilles' heels) and, as a result, repeat our mistakes and make ourselves even more vulnerable. "Rather than accepting his vulnerability and learning from it," writes Dr. Bloomfield, "Achilles defiantly sought to prove he was invincible. He repeatedly exposed himself to attack." Either Achilles was oblivious to his weak spot or he was indulging in a mighty act of denial. Either way, he left his heel unprotected.

Dr. Bloomfield thinks we lesser mortals do exactly the same thing with our psychological deficiencies and imperfections. Being human, we all have shortcomings that can impair our relationships, our careers, and our personal growth. And, being

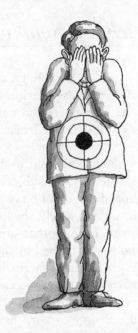

human, we tend to deny or resist them, and this gives rise to the Achilles Syndrome.

The essence of the syndrome, and its central paradox, is this: the more you resist your Achilles' heel, the more it persists. According to Dr. Bloomfield, if you deny your weak spots or try to prove that they don't exist, you actually reinforce the psychological mechanisms that caused the weaknesses in the first place, since you won't change what you don't acknowledge to be dysfunctional. Furthermore, the energy we spend concealing our vulnerabilities from other people, not to mention from ourselves, usually constitutes a bigger psychological burden than the limitation we are trying to resist in the first place.

Achilles' heels are not necessarily pathological states or deep-seated psychoses. They are merely imperfections to which we all are heir, such as the fear of getting hurt in relationships, insecurity about our physical appearances, or being terrified of criticism. In each case, denying your fear can make you behave in such a way as to create situations in which what you fear actually happens.

Some people think they have no Achilles' heels. Their Achilles' heel is probably an irrational need to think they are perfect, and that too induces the syndrome. If your need to be flawless is strong enough, you will drive your weaknesses from your awareness altogether, leaving yourself foolishly unprotected, like a boxer with slurred speech and wobbly knees and blood dripping into his eyes who tells his handlers he's ready to go back into the ring and nail his opponent.

The metaffect is a reminder of the high price we pay for fooling ourselves. If you find yourself refusing to acknowledge your own flaws and foibles, perhaps having this term in your lexicon can change your internal monologues: "Stop kidding yourself, Big Guy. Face reality. You don't want to end up like Achilles."

The term can also be expanded beyond Dr. Bloomfield's psychiatric definition, to other forms of denial, or to those times when you are lulled into a false sense of security. Here are some sample uses:

"You keep insisting those chest pains are merely indigestion. But if you don't let a cardiologist check them out, your death certificate might read 'Cause of death: Achilles Syndrome.'"

"Slow down, Achilles. I don't care how well this car handles; you're not invulnerable."

"You're totally oblivious to financial reality. If you keep flashing credit cards around, your creditors won't have mercy just because you're afflicted with the Achilles Syndrome."

"They should rename that team the Achilles Syndrome. Every time they get a comfortable lead they slack off as if they can't lose, and the next thing you know, they're playing like they have arrows in their heels."

Naturally, you can also use the term to help other people. The next time someone denies that he or she has a tendency toward arrogance, self-pity, crabbiness, deceit, or any of a thousand human frailties, you will have a fresh way of encouraging honest self-reflection: "Please don't be offended, but I feel I owe it to you to bring something to your attention. See, there's something called the Achilles Syndrome. . . ." (In fact, you might find such a civilized approach especially useful if your own Achilles' heel is the tendency to criticize others with rash or offensive statements. If you don't phrase your objections discreetly, someone is liable to shoot an arrow right into your impertinence.)

The Alienation Effect

The German dramatist and poet Bertolt Brecht was known for writing politically charged plays such as *The Threepenny Opera* and *Mother Courage*. A controversial figure, Brecht was as radical in his approach to theater as he was in his politics. Concerned with instruction as well as entertainment, his "epic theater" employed a variety of theatrical devices geared to shock his audience into the recognition of social and political injustices in Europe early in this century. In addition, Brecht used sets and lighting to reveal to spectators various elements of the staging process itself, in essence reminding them that they were, in fact, watching a show.

Brecht wanted the audience to preserve a state of intellectual detachment from the play, because, in his words, "the more the public was emotionally affected, the less capable it was of learning." He called this principle the *Alienation Effect*.

Don't lose yourself in the play, the dramatist was saying, don't give in to the theatrical illusion, don't identify too closely with what the characters are doing. Keep your distance, remain objective. Brecht's philosophy was the antithesis of the classic, Aristotelian approach to drama, in which the actor imitates the hero and the spectator mentally imitates the actor, thus psychologically partaking of the hero's experience. According to Aristotelian theory, by feeling the same fear, or pity, or whatever emotions the character portrays, the spectator thereby undergoes *catharsis,* a purging of those emotions, and is able to return to life with renewed strength. But Brecht felt that European audiences between world wars needed the more dispassionate, objective experience of the Alienation Effect.

Of course, the word *alienation* has acquired negative, even pathological connotations, suggesting a condition of being an outsider, isolated or estranged from one's surroundings. Indeed, the word's roots, the French *aliéné* and the Spanish *alienado,* originally meant "insane." Brecht used the term in a more positive vein. In his view, "to alienate an event or a character is simply to take what to the event or character is obvious, known, evident and produce surprise and curiosity out of it."

Brecht's ultimate purpose was to create drama that was both illuminating and entertaining, which sounds like a pretty good way to approach life in general, not just theater. To the extent that life is a play (and no less an expert than William Shakespeare has told us, "All the world's a stage, and all the men and women merely players"), it is not too big a stretch to apply the term "Alienation Effect" to everyday experience.

At certain times, it might be useful to invoke the metaffect as a reminder to be a detached spectator in the play of life. Crises, tragedies, and sudden shocks force us to make quick evaluations and crucial decisions even though our perceptions are muddy and our judgment is overshadowed by emotion. At such times, you want your mind to remain clear even though your emotions and senses are muddled by the drama, thus achieving a shift in gears similar to that which Brecht sought to induce in his audience.

For example, the metaffect can help you get through mundane annoyances that induce not healthy catharsis but toxic stress. You're stuck on the freeway gagging on exhaust fumes; you're at the check-out counter with a carton of milk and the person in front of you has enough in her cart to feed an army, but she won't let you go first; the family in the Winnebago is turning your idyllic weekend into the camping trip from hell. At such times you want to strive for the Alienation Effect. Get yourself off the stage and watch the show as if it's all a comedy.

Or, consider a crisis at work. Your company has just launched a product that sank like a torpedoed ship. The boss is about to replace the whole marketing staff, eliminate research and development, and cancel all vacations. You calmly enter his office and say, "Listen, J.R., this situation calls for the Alienation Effect. Why don't you take a minute to pull yourself together. Step back, get off the stage, and look at this little setback as if you were a spectator."

The term has another level of metaffective potential if one considers Brecht's exhortation to "take what is obvious, known or evident and [produce] surprise and curiosity out of it." This hints at seeing the world afresh, as might an alien. Who wouldn't benefit from such a refreshing and transformative perspective? "Look, we've been to Paris so many times we're getting jaded. This time, let's strive for the Alienation Effect. Try to see the place as if we were Martians landing on the Eiffel Tower for the first time."

Taking the concept to another level, the Alienation Effect suggests a kind of Buddhist detachment. Eastern sages counsel aspirants to separate themselves psychologically from the material world because the temporary pleasures of the senses are miniscule compared to the bliss of spiritual union. Detachment in this sense entails the seemingly paradoxical trick of combining joyous participation in the world with an inner contentment untouched by joy or sorrow. As this state of consciousness is also said to be the most receptive to wisdom, one could say that one who attains it has achieved in life what Brecht hoped to provide for theatergoers: a detachment that both enlightens and entertains.

The next time life seems to glow with newfound freshness and your inner domain is marked by wisdom and peace, call your friends and tell them you've glimpsed the meaning of life and it's called the Alienation Effect.

The Autokinetic Effect

In order to understand what psychologists call the *Autokinetic Effect,* you can darken your room entirely, except for a single small light, such as the power indicator on a stereo. If you watch that point of light long enough, it will probably seem to move, perhaps traveling erratically in different directions.

In experiments the effect works almost every time, even when the person viewing the light *knows* it is not actually moving. You might even feel uncertain about the stability of your own position in space, particularly if you are in a chair without a back or are unfamiliar with the room.

The Autokinetic Effect was known to astronomers long before experimental psychologists named it. On a dark, cloudy night when there is only a single source of light, such as a beacon or a star, that light will appear to move around. One needs a point of reference in order to localize the source of light with any degree of certainty.

As a metaffect, this term aptly describes several common illusions: perceiving movement where none actually exists, misconstruing the location of things, and believing something is happening when it's actually occurring only in one's mind. Just as a person in a dark room can think a light is moving when it's not, cut off from familiar conditions, we can get so confused psychologically that we become prone to misperceptions and errors of judgment. When we are disoriented, unsure of the true feelings of other people or of the nature of events unfolding outside the range of our antennae, a metaffective Autokinetic Effect can make us leap to an erroneous conclusion or misjudge our own positions.

For example, you might think a particular business deal in a foreign country (or even in a new area of enterprise) is moving ahead in a desired direction, only to discover that it is not moving anywhere. It instead has become stagnant or fallen apart completely. You might say, "Damn! All along, I thought we were getting close to making a deal, and it turns out to be an Autokinetic Effect."

Consider the application to love. Have you ever felt a new relationship was moving along splendidly, carrying you into exciting unexplored territory, only to discover that the other person had no such perception, that in fact he or she did not think the relationship was making progress at all and saw no future in it? In the aftermath, you can come to some understanding of what really happened: "No need to be depressed. I thought we had a good thing going, but it turned out to be just one of those autokinetic affairs."

On the other hand, have you ever started a platonic friendship with someone you liked, only to discover that he or she was hoping to move in a romantic direction? You might say, "Look, I don't want to hurt you, but I think we have an Autokinetic Effect on our hands."

Some other uses of this versatile metaffect:

(At work) "I thought I knew exactly where I was going with this research project, but it's taken on a life of its own and now I don't know where I'm at. I must have been befuddled by some kind of Autokinetic Effect."

(On the road) "This was no Autokinetic Effect, officer. That other car was definitely changing lanes."

(At the singles bar) "I don't believe it. Am I going through some kind of autokinetic thing or is that hunk actually coming over to talk to me?"

Whenever you are in unfamiliar territory, remember the possibility of autokinetic dislocation and check your bearings with someone who can help you to see in the dark!

The Babinski Reflex

If you stroke the outside of a baby's foot from the little toe down toward the heel, you will notice that its big toe jerks upward and the other toes splay. This is an involuntary response, first described in 1896 by the French neurologist Joseph François Felix Babinski, who was rewarded by having his name given to the phenomenon. You are not likely to observe the *Babinski Reflex* once a child is walking and talking, however, because at around eighteen months the reaction becomes inhibited by the developing higher brain centers.

In contrast to humans, apes exhibit the Babinski Reflex at all ages, not just early childhood. Why does it disappear in growing humans but persist in our primate cousins? Some scientists postulate that the reflex is useful for grasping and releasing the branches of trees, a distinct advantage to apes but not so pertinent to humans. The mechanism that inhibits this reflex, they believe, developed late in the evolution of primates, when our early ancestors forsook trees to walk on the ground.

Metaffectively, then, the Babinski Reflex can be considered a vestigial reaction left over from a more primitive state. Think of it as an atavism that humans ought to get over by the time they are two years old (or at least by adolescence) and that only beasts retain into adulthood. We all have metaphoric Babinski Reflexes, of course, and some of them are rather useful: for example, attacking someone who threatens your child, or running away from a rabid dog, or experiencing the stirring in the loins when the first scent of spring tickles the mating instinct ("Man, she brings out the beast in me! One look at her and I babinski like a dog in heat"). These are primitive reflexes we can be glad we've retained.

Then there are socially unacceptable Babinski Reflexes, those personality traits and irrational actions that smack of regrettable reversions to a more primitive ancestral state—the sort of behavior that might move you to call the perpetrator an ape. These include temper tantrums and rage reactions induced by a trivial offense, barroom brawls ignited by a careless remark or a suggestive look at another person's date, mating rituals that fall just shy of clubbing a woman over the head and hauling her off to a cave, and various forms of savagery on the freeways and subways of America.

With Babinski on the tip of your tongue, you have a metaffect of many colors with which to describe brutes, hoodlums, and oafs. When gang warfare erupts, you can remark, "These kids are going to Babinski themselves to an early grave."

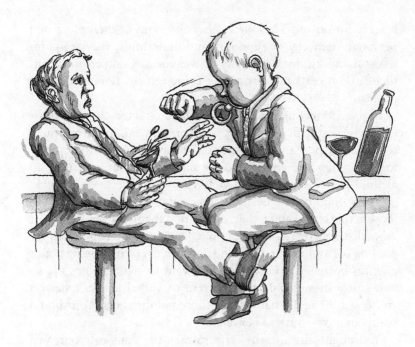

You can refer to a friend whose behavior needs a defense with, "Don't mind him. He means no harm. He's just having one of his Babinski Reflexes."

To better describe what sociologists have labeled "British Disease"—hooligans rioting at soccer games—you can say, "Thousands were injured today when a large group of Liverpool partisans jerked to a collective Babinski Reflex."

You will also find ample use for the term if you associate with the sort of authoritarian personalities who have what pioneering psychologist Abraham Maslow termed a "jungle outlook." Those possessing this primitive world view, said Maslow, see existence as a jungle, "in which [each] man's hand is necessarily against every other man's. . . . The whole world is conceived of as dangerous, threatening, or at least challenging." Such people tend to be suspicious, hostile, anxious, and hungry for power. They view others in terms of their place in a personal hierarchy of superiors and underlings; they see compassion and kindness as signs of weakness. Competition, conflicts, and threats to their power bring out the Babinski Reflex in them.

If you are feeling brave, when such characters act in a brutish, belligerent, domineering manner, you might throw them off balance, perhaps even shock them back to civility, by saying, "Lighten up, you ape. Your Babinski Reflex is acting up again." Then be prepared to yield to your own reflex and duck.

There might even be times when you deliberately want to loosen the constraints that our rational minds place on our animalistic instincts. For example, let's say your employees are goofing off and making all kinds of careless errors. Being a nice guy has gotten you nowhere. You want to shake things up, so you storm in and unleash a torrent of verbal abuse. Later on you boast, "I really babinskied those goldbrickers. You should see them now—busy as beavers."

You might also use the term to take the onus off your own impulsive behavior. Say you're at a restaurant with your wife when a gorgeous blond wiggles past your table. As your eyes follow every jiggle and bounce, you feel the sharp sting of your wife's stiletto heel on your toe. Now you can apologize by saying, "I'm sorry, dear, it was just a Babinski Reflex."

Or, perhaps you're a woman nursing a drink, minding your own business. Suddenly, your nostrils quiver at the scent of too much Aqua Velva. A self-anointed wild-and-crazy guy is hovering over you. "Hi there, sexy," he oozes. "Come here often?" You politely explain that you'd like to be alone. He won't buy it. Slithering within an inch of your face, he pours out his full repertoire of repugnant come-ons; when you less-than-politely tell him to bug off, he informs you that, in his humble opinion, you are a stuck-up bitch. As he wipes the contents of your drink from his eyes and checks his lip for blood, you can say, "Excuse me. I just don't seem to have my Babinski Reflexes under control."

The Bambiology Syndrome

In the spring of 1988, trainers at the San Diego Wild Animal Park were reprimanded for disciplining an elephant cow named Dunda. The trainers had judged that Dunda had become unmanageable and represented a significant threat to her keepers and other animals, so they disciplined her with beatings. However, the punishment was deemed excessive by zoo caretakers; the elephant had suffered debilitating wounds. When word got out, there was a huge uproar. Most of the press coverage was predictably lurid, the general impression being that Dunda had been brutalized by sadists. The trainers received hundreds of hate letters and the Zoological Society was besieged with canceled memberships and demands for swift, and in some cases draconian, punishment.

Setting aside the question of guilt and innocence, what is of interest here is a phrase used in the defense of the trainers' action. Those accused of brutality labeled the press coverage yellow journalism and claimed that thrashing Dunda was an appropriate professional decision, made in the best interests of an intractable animal for whom euthanasia may have been the only alternative. One of the defendants, trainer Alan Roocroft, attributed the public outcry to a phenomenon he called the *Bambiology Syndrome*.

The Bambiology Syndrome, Roocroft explains, consists of a tendency to anthropomorphize animals, that is, to attribute to them the qualities of a human being, such as a sense of humor, much as cartoonists have done over the years; hence the allusion to Disney's adorable, heart-rending fawn. The effect of the syndrome, in Roocroft's view, is to sentimentalize animals and to romanticize the "unspoiled" state of nature. Many bambiologists seem to think the only difference between animals and humans is who pays to see whom at the zoo.

Those afflicted with the syndrome have an excessively idealized view of nature. Their image of the natural world is probably a place where blue jays and butterflies flutter against a warm azure sky and deer and antelope frolic in fields of daisies. Ignored is the side of life in the wild that Alfred Lord Tennyson described as "Nature, red in tooth and claw," a wholesale slaughterhouse where most creatures are some other creature's lunch and where the hazards are considerably more rugged than fending off mosquitoes at a picnic.

Readers of this book, like its author, no doubt love animals and are opposed to cruelty. No doubt we all revere nature. Nor is there doubt that we all want to see justice done if Dunda the elephant was indeed brutalized. However, one can worship at the altar of nature without gushing with sentimentality or blinding oneself to certain ruthless realities, which are, upon reflection, no less wondrous and awe-inspiring than pretty pastel landscapes or snapshots of adorable seals bouncing balls on their noses. One can love animals without turning the critters into mute humans. But for those who go to anthropomorphic extremes, we now have an evocative metaffect in the Bambiology Syndrome.

To whom would the term apply? You might attach it to people who dress their poodles in cute little outfits better

suited to children, or to animal lovers whose more-sensitive-than-thou demeanor turns the rest of us red in tooth and claw, or to latter-day Thoreaus who boast about being close to nature when the closest they come to the wild is peering through the windows of their Winnebagos, or to pet owners who treat Fido and Fifi better than their own kids: "Do we have to go to their party? That whole family has the Bambiology Syndrome. The way they talk to those performing pets!"

The Bandwagon Effect

Return with us now to the days of yesteryear, before the advent of sound bites and media consultants and spin doctors, when campaigning for votes was a more direct art. At election time it was customary, especially in the South, for parades to march through town led by a brass band aboard a long wagon. The parades were meant to call the public's attention to a rally or give them a firsthand look at a smiling, hat-waving candidate. Frequently, some local leader would climb aboard the wagon and ride with the band, thus identifying himself with the cause at hand and propping up his stature in the eyes of his aroused constituents.

In this manner did the familiar phrase "climb on the bandwagon" enter the American lexicon at the turn of the century, during William Jennings Bryan's second failed campaign for the presidency. It means, essentially, to show support for a popular trend with the intention of profiting from it.

Later, psychologists borrowed the expression to define an empirical discovery that perceptive laypersons have observed on their own. The *Bandwagon Effect* is the tendency of some people to withhold their opinions until they know the majority's view, at which time they merrily announce that they feel exactly the way almost everyone else does. The effect is apparently caused by a combination of weakly held opinions and the need to find security in numbers. In both laboratory experiments and actual voting situations, it is quite common for people to actually switch positions when it turns out that the majority is on the other side.

Although the phenomenon is old and familiar, the formal, scientific term has metaffective value for us today. The media's current infatuation with poll-taking has probably already made the Bandwagon Effect a significant factor in public life. In an age in which samples of the population are polled about everything from Academy Awards to foreign policy, and when pundits make daily assessments of the prevailing wisdom, there is a real danger that collective Bandwagon Effects will influence the public agenda. Perhaps more ominous, the bandwagon that people climb aboard can very well be bogus, created by an erroneous reading of public opinion. When told that the "majority" holds a certain view, large numbers of people have embraced a position without thinking the issue through, thus actually creating a majority where none existed.

In the summer of 1989, for example, in response to a Supreme Court ruling, a few zealous legislators began calling for a ban on desecrating the American flag. Their colleagues were so afraid of appearing unpatriotic that they voiced only feeble opposition, and most jumped on the bandwagon, no doubt inspired by opinion polls suggesting that Americans wanted to protect Old Glory. As a result, the flag issue received more attention and passionate debate than the environment, the budget deficit, or the unprecedented social changes taking place in Eastern Europe.

Bandwagoning can be a convenient way to escape ambivalence and avoid hard thinking. It is certainly more comfortable than maintaining a deviant position. Knowing the term for the phenomenon might help us guard against it with more vigilance. Perhaps responsible news editors will tell their reporters, "Be sure to make it clear that this is only one opinion. We don't want to create a Bandwagon Effect by suggesting that most people feel this way."

Unfortunately, the news media can be victims, not just perpetrators, of the Bandwagon Effect. Wrote the *Los Angeles Times*, "Increasingly, it seems, a media consensus forms on major events quicker than you can say 'pack journalism.' Critics say such consensus journalism is both more prevalent and more perilous than ever before." There evidently are several reasons that news is becoming more and more uniform: reporters all talk to same sources; the demand for speed and brevity discourages reflection and independent investigation; and journalists are afraid to be out of step with their colleagues, because being wrong might damage their careers. Hence, once an event becomes public, journalists start to bandwagon and the story gets the same spin by everyone.

We were all misled by a journalistic Bandwagon Effect in the spring of 1989, when advocates of democracy flooded the streets of Beijing. Reporters and expert commentators, perhaps swept away by wishful thinking and a lust for drama, bandwagoned the conviction that the democracy movement in China was irreversible. Then the tanks rolled into Tiananmen Square, crushing the demonstrators and the bandwagon alike.

Still, the metaffect has utility in many areas of everyday life. Consider business: an important issue has been raised in your office; everyone is debating the matter and forming opinions. You feel strongly about your views, but you discover, as the moment of decision nears, that a number of colleagues have adopted the opposite position. Knowing this metaffect, you might want to get opinions in private, one at a time, and to caution others: "Let's get an accurate reading of everyone's views right now, before the Bandwagon Effect takes over."

Suppose a friend and supporter deserts your side and goes over to the alleged majority. Dealing with such an annoying and disheartening turnabout can be difficult. Now you can say, "Poor guy, he succumbed to the Bandwagon Effect." It's so much more civilized, gracious, and erudite than, "That gutless, brown-nosing traitor wimped out on me!"

On the other hand, if you have a Machiavellian bent, you can use your knowledge of this metaffect to advantage: "Look, you and I know we're right, and everyone else either doesn't care or doesn't know what he wants. So, let's spread the word that everyone agrees with us and we'll get a Bandwagon Effect going."

The metaffect can also be a useful teaching tool for parents of teenagers, the group most biologically disposed to bandwagoning. I have a friend whose fourteen-year-old was very upset because, try as she may, she just did not like Michael Jackson. The father might have said, "Sweetheart, there's nothing wrong with having a minority opinion. I'll bet lots of kids don't like Michael Jackson, but they're afraid to admit it. Let me tell you about the Bandwagon Effect."

The metaffect can apply to any herdlike behavior, not just to opinions. Fads and fashions and trendiness in general are bandwagon phenomena, aided and abetted by advertising. "Wait a minute! Why are we buying this? I don't even *like* radicchio, and these miniature vegetables look like dollhouse food. Aren't we getting caught up in some yuppie Bandwagon Effect?"

Of course, not all bandwagons are bad. The ardent voices of respected figures can sometimes move public opinion in a decidedly honorable direction. A decade ago, ecology activists were voices in the wilderness, viewed by the mainstream as weirdos, extremists, or doomsaying alarmists; today, a clean environment is, next to drugs, the public's number-one concern. Similarly, in the 1950s and early 1960s, civil-rights advocates were troublemakers who were impertinent enough to call attention to an ugly blemish on the American Dream. Thanks largely to a Bandwagon Effect stimulated by the Johnson administration and the Supreme Court, nondiscrimination has become mainstream policy. Sometimes one can take pride in being a bandwagonier.

The Barnum Effect

He was the archetypal American showman, a marketing genius who invented hype long before it was polished into an art form by Madison Avenue and Hollywood. He started in 1835, at age twenty-five, when he purchased an 80-year-old slave and billed her as the 161-year-old former nurse of George Washington. He went on to exhibit freaks and phony monsters, bringing in huge crowds with ballyhoo and bogus claims, and he crowned it all by creating the circus he called "The Greatest Show on Earth." The quote books immortalize Phineas Taylor Barnum for his famous remark, "There's a sucker born every minute."

For this insight into the human condition, Barnum had a psychological phenomenon named after him by psychologist Paul Meehl. The *Barnum Effect* has to do with the tendency of people to accept as accurate, for them personally, a generalized statement (especially a flattering one) that might in fact characterize just about anyone.

Here's how the effect was demonstrated in research. First, psychologists set up conditions in which subjects were interviewed or given a battery of tests. Later, the subjects were given a report, said to be based on a systematic, rigorous analysis of the test data. The reports were not personalized assessments at all, however, but were written before the tests were even administered and featured such generalized statements as "You have a strong need for other people to like you" or "Sexual adjustment has presented some problems for you." Furthermore, every subject was given the identical report. Each time the experiment is conducted, the great majority of participants are impressed by how accurately their personalities have been captured.

As a metaffect, the Barnum Effect can be used whenever

someone abandons critical thinking because he wants to believe what he hears. Suppose a friend of yours gets carried away by something said by a fortune-teller or palm reader or a newspaper astrology column. "Maybe I should cancel that meeting with the broker," he says. "I'm supposed to be very cautious in financial transactions today." You might reply, "Hey, *everyone* should be cautious *every* day. Don't let yourself get barnumed by that charlatan."

As a metaffective malarkey detector, the concept is perfect for dealing with phonies. When someone tries to impress you with uncanny insight into your essential nature by saying something like, "You seem so competent and self-assured, but I sense a deep vulnerability in you. You've been hurt in the past, haven't you?" the red flags should go up in your brain: Barnum Effect! Barnum Effect!

Are you hiring someone? Watch out for the candidate who comes in and offers trenchant observations such as "I sense that you'd like to increase your profit margin and get more out of your advertising dollar. I'm the man to do it."

Respond with, "Thank you, Mr. Barnum. Don't call us, we'll call you."

Of course, you can use the Barnum Effect to advantage. There are any number of business situations in which to say, "Set up a luncheon meeting. I'll see if I can barnum those guys into our way of thinking."

Or, suppose there's someone at a party you want to impress. You can combine flattery with barnumation by saying, "I'll bet no one knows the real you. Beneath your sophistication and competence, I sense there's a playful little child in you."

Then hope that the person you're attracted to is one of the suckers who was born that particular minute.

Bell's Theorem

In the early part of this century, nuclear physicists overturned the model of the universe that had been sacrosanct since the days of Isaac Newton. Amazed scientists discovered the world of Quantum Mechanics, where subatomic particles are somehow not just particles but also waves, and physicists, with all their high-tech gadgetry, can't make measurements or predictions that are anything more than statistical approximations. Quantum mechanics offered a mind-boggling vision of the substructure of matter, and it called into question the very nature of what we call reality.

Like most revolutions, this one stirred up passion. In the early thirties, a fierce debate raged over the proper interpretation of quantum phenomena. One view was the co-called Copenhagen Interpretation championed by Niels Bohr. It stated, essentially, that there is no reality until that reality is perceived, and our perception of reality will always appear somewhat contradictory, unpredictable, and paradoxical. On the other side was Albert Einstein, who abhorred Bohr's interpretation. Asserting that God does not play dice with the universe, he proposed that there were "hidden variables" governing subatomic events that, once discovered, would render even the subatomic realm as predictable as the behavior of large, everyday objects.

To prove his point, Einstein and two colleagues, Boris Podolsky and Nathan Rosen, constructed a thought experiment designed to prove that quantum mechanics must be regarded as incomplete and therefore require a different interpretation. The resulting paper, published in 1935, was as controversial as it was brilliant. It sought to prove that when followed to its logical conclusion, quantum mechanics predicts illogical results and contradicts itself.

To illustrate this point, the authors invented a hypothetical situation involving a particle that explodes into two fragments, both of which travel undisturbed to opposite ends of the universe. If the quantum model is true, the paper demonstrated, then the two fragments would somehow have to remain in communication with each other. This became known as the *EPR Effect,* after the initials of the three scientists.

To Einstein and his collaborators, this thought experiment proved the absurdity of the Copenhagen Interpretation because of a universally accepted proposition in physics: the principle of local causes, which states that what happens in one area does not depend on variables in another area. Since phenomena are by nature localized, Einstein concluded, there must be a serious flaw in quantum theory.

However, in 1964 John Stewart Bell, a physicist at the European Organization for Nuclear Research (CERN) in Switzerland, proved Einstein wrong and Bohr right. In a mathematical proof that came to be called *Bell's Theorem,* Bell used hypothetical conditions similar to the EPR experiment and proved essentially this: if the statistical predictions of quantum theory are valid, then the principle of local causes is false. And, since quantum theory's statistical predictions have been proved valid time and again, phenomena are *not* in fact dependent on local causes alone. Events are influenced by what happens at a distance. "If this explanation is correct," writes Gary Zukav in his overview of the new physics, *The Dancing Wu Li Masters,* "then we live in a nonlocal universe . . . characterized by superluminal (faster-than-light) connections between apparently 'separate parts.' "

The theorem could be taken to mean that there are really no separate parts in the universe; regardless of distance, everything is connected in an intimate and immediate way. To some, this deep level of interconnection and communication between objects separated by distance justifies a belief in psychic phenomena such as telepathy and extrasensory perception. This interpretation is rich with metaffective possibilities. Suppose you suddenly think about your friend Steve, who is hundreds of miles away, and an instant later the phone rings. You answer, "Hello, Steve? . . . I knew it was you! Hey, if we work on this, maybe we can communicate for free with Bell's Theorem instead of giving our money to Bell Telephone."

Or perhaps you just "know" that something bad is happening to your brother, and the next day you find out that something bad had indeed happened at the very time you had that feeling. Now, when you tell your friends about such inexplicable occurrences and they scoffingly compare you to Shirley MacLaine, you can counter with a bona-fide scientific term: "It's no big deal, really. It's explained by Bell's Theorem."

The concept can also take some of the sting out of separations. The next time you leave on a long business trip, tell your lover, "Don't be sad. Distance can't really separate us. Our hearts will communicate like two EPR particles, hooked up eternally by Bell's Theorem."

If you have children, you can use the metaffect as a parenting device. If your teenager wants to go to an unsupervised party, you can say, "Listen, kiddo, you can forget about trying to fool me. I'll *know* what you're doing. Bell's Theorem means that my mind is inextricably connected to yours."

The metaffect is particularly handy to explain unaccountable phenomena, such as the discovery by simply everyone in the office that the boss is turning down your pet project before you have even left the meeting in which he told you first. We all know that light travels faster than sound; Bell's Theorem suggests that information can travel faster than light.

The Biffle Poll

When President Franklin Delano Roosevelt died in office in April 1945, Vice President Harry S Truman reportedly asked Mrs. Roosevelt if there was anything he could do for her. Replied the widowed First Lady, "Is there anything *we* can do for *you?* For you are the one in trouble now."

Indeed, the new President had his hands full. He had to conclude World War II, preside over the Marshall Plan and the conversion to a peacetime economy, and contend with the early days of the Cold War, all in the formidable shadow of a revered leader who had seen the country through the Great Depression and the war.

The next three years were rough going for Truman. His popularity sank so low that, in midterm elections, the opposition Republicans gained control of both houses of Congress for the first time since 1930 and members of his own party asked him to resign. As the 1948 presidential campaign approached, prominent Democrats searched desperately for a more popular candidate, even courting Dwight D. Eisenhower for a while. When they settled for Truman, the incumbent's support was so lukewarm that signs at the convention declared, "We're Just Mild About Harry."

Running against New York governor Thomas E. Dewey, Truman was a big underdog. Democrats bolted from the party; former Vice President Henry A. Wallace ran on the Progressive party ticket and Strom Thurmond organized a State's Rights party that attracted Southerners opposed to Truman's civil-rights policies. A Dewey landslide was so taken for granted that pollster George Gallup, when asked to take a survey for the Republicans, turned the job down, contending that "the results are a foregone conclusion."

The expert predictions were so consistent that bookmakers set odds as high as 18 to 1 in favor of Dewey. Only one member of the National Press Club predicted a Democratic victory: Harry S Truman himself. But, undaunted, the President set out on a 31,000-mile whistle-stop campaign, predicting an upset. What made him so confident in the face of such massive disagreement? Was it merely faith? Was it a survival mechanism? No, it was the *Biffle Poll.*

Lester Biffle, the secretary of the Senate and a Truman supporter, had his doubts about the "scientific polls," so he decided to conduct an informal survey of his own. According to political scientist Richard M. Pious, author of *The American Presidency,* Biffle disguised himself as a chicken peddler and went from neighborhood to neighborhood asking ordinary citizens how they planned to vote. When he was satisfied that he had plumbed the true feelings of the electorate, he reportedly told Truman, "Listen, Harry, you don't have to worry."

On election night, with the Deep South turning to Strom Thurmond and Dewey taking New York, the *Chicago Tribune* went to press with its infamous headline: DEWEY DEFEATS TRUMAN. But "Give 'em Hell Harry" had given 'em such hell that he nabbed 303 electoral votes to Dewey's 189, and his coattails swept the Democrats back into majorities in the House and Senate. The Biffle Poll turned out to be the only accurate gauge of the country's real mood.

Remember the Biffle Poll as a metaffect for turning to your own sources of information when formal methods (such as polls and market surveys) are unsatisfactory. In some respects, it's a safety device against the Bandwagon Effect. You need not dress up as a chicken peddler, but there are times when an informal, biffle-type grass-roots inquiry might yield more reliable information than the untested conventional wisdom, or at least information of a different nature.

The stock market is heavily influenced by the biffling of

rumors, gossip, and speculation along the Wall Street grapevine. And, in every industry, many top-level executives rely heavily on "soft data" such as hearsay, casual conversations, and idle speculation to get a bead on what's really going on in the marketplace or in their own companies. Some go biffling in the employee cafeteria, for example, to learn what average people are thinking.

Consider the following scenario. Your crack marketing team displays sophisticated charts and graphs illustrating exactly why the public will not support your new product line. Based on their presentation, your accountants conclude that the data demand that you scrap the project. But your gut tells you there's more to be known about the situation. You dismiss the naysayers and call in your trusted aide: "Jane, let's biffle this on our own. Snoop around the department stores, chat it up with the consumers, talk to people on the commuter train. Find out how the real people feel."

The metaffect is also a perfect way to explain a Truman-esque conviction when the odds seem stacked against you. Entrepreneurs now have a term they can use in front of a cadre of high-powered bankers and financiers. Suppose your great idea for a chain of guava-juice stands has been met with barely disguised cynicism. You can tell your advisers, "I know you think I'll lose a fortune, but I don't care. My internal Biffle Poll tells me that The Guava Haven will be a big success."

If they don't believe you, tell them about Truman and Lester Biffle—or about Ray Kroc, whose inner biffle meter told him to defy the experts and franchise McDonald's.

The Boomerang Effect

Did you ever try to persuade someone to change his mind only to have him assert his original position more strongly than before? Have you ever been presented with information contrary to what you believed in and responded to the input by becoming even more adamant in your opposition? If so, you have experienced firsthand what psychologists call the *Boomerang Effect,* in the first instance as a victim, in the second as an exemplar.

The Boomerang Effect, in a sense the opposite of the Bandwagon Effect, is defined as the phenomenon in which attempts to change attitudes in a particular direction produce shifts in the direction opposite that intended. Psychologists are not quite sure why the boomerang occurs sometimes and not others, but the fact that the effect is strongest when the message embodies a powerful emotional appeal suggests that defensiveness is most aroused when values and feelings are attacked.

Now you have an established term with which to label a rather common occurrence. The next time a group uses vehement emotional appeals to try to censor a movie or book—as when various organizations picketed *The Last Temptation of Christ* or when an Ayatollah puts a price on the head of someone who has offended him—you will know what to call it when the public reacts in exactly the opposite direction. (Most books targeted for banning would probably be read by only a handful of literati if not for the publicity engendered by would-be censors, and films such as *The Last Temptation* draw thousands more to the box office than they would have without the controversy.)

Closer to home, you will want to watch out for boomerangs in your relationships. Suppose you and your mate are arguing over some highly charged issue, each party's vehemence rising in direct proportion to the other's, until the whole thing escalates to a level of furor far in excess of anyone's actual feelings. Knowing this metaffect, you might now be able to catch yourself before the boomerang flies back into your faces: "Honey, what started all that anyway? I don't really care that much, do you? We have to curb these Boomerang Effects."

Parents of teenagers are especially vulnerable to boomerangs, since their offspring tend to do exactly what they are told not to do. Rather than force Bach or Miles Davis on your rock-loving teenagers in an effort to raise their musical tastes, you can find out the names of the hottest heavy-metal bands, buy a few of their records, and play the music day and night. Faster than a Vladimir Horowitz arpeggio, your teens will be ready for a change of genre.

(Actually, music may be the least of your boomerang concerns. Studies show that romantic attraction increases when parents try to keep lovers apart. They have a name for that too: the Romeo and Juliet Effect.)

The next time your business colleagues respond to a sensible argument by doing exactly the opposite, or by asserting their own views with unwarranted aggressiveness, you might find this a useful metaffect: "Fellow members of the board, I greatly respect your judgment. However, I've concluded that your views on this matter are a result of a Boomerang Effect, so I'm going to do it my way."

Of course, if you're wily enough, you can use the Boomerang Effect to advantage. Take the lead of Les, a real-estate salesman I know. When a prospective buyer is on the fence about a purchase, Les says, "This isn't the right place for you. Perhaps we should look at something in another price range." Les has sold a lot of property to boomerangers.

Boyle's Law

Things are closing in around you. Deadlines are looming, debts are mounting, competitors are coiled to attack, and your boss is making excessive demands. It feels as if your range of action is increasingly restricted and your options are steadily diminishing. The pressure inside you is building up in direct proportion to oppressive outside events. You are about to burst. Metaphorically speaking, you have become a victim of *Boyle's Law*.

A giant in the history of science, Robert Boyle labored in laboratories in Oxford and London, making major contributions to the revolutionary theories associated with his contemporary, Sir Isaac Newton. Boyle gave us the first precise definitions of the chemical element, the chemical reaction, and chemical analysis—achievements that earned him the sobriquet "father of modern chemistry." He also invented the vacuum pump and used it to discover the law that bears his name.

Boyle's Law explains the relationship between gas volume and pressure. Essentially, it states that, at a constant temperature, the pressure of a quantity of gas is inversely proportional to its volume. Suppose you have a container with a given amount of gas inside. If you keep the temperature constant and reduce the volume of the container by half—perhaps by moving the walls closer—the pressure exerted by the gas will double. If you reduce the volume of the container to a third of its original size the pressure will triple, if you decrease it to a fourth it will quadruple, and so on, as long as you do not change the temperature. If you make it hotter or cooler, the pressure behaves in an entirely different manner and Boyle's Law is inoperative.

As a metaffect, Boyle's Law can refer to pressure of a more human kind. When circumstances close in on us, our nerve cells and vital organs respond and we experience a proportional increase in tension. Now, instead of simply telling your boss, "I'm under stress," which sounds pedestrian, or muttering, "I have a lot of pressure on me," which sounds both obvious and complaining, you can respond with a knowledgeable remark that suggests you paid attention during science classes: "Okay, Shirley, I'll do it your way, but mark my words, the Boyle's Law conditions you are imposing are only going to make matters worse." Or you might remind a colleague who gets a report on your desk just a minute before you are supposed to approve it, "You know, Throckmorton, even I am subject to Boyle's Law and you have just cut my volume to zero. Watch out that I don't explode."

The metaffect is not only more culturally literate than the alternatives but also has much greater precision. For example, suppose a deadline is moved up from four weeks to two, or the opposing team cuts your lead from six points to three. Now you can declare, "According to my Boyle's Law meter, the pressure on us has just doubled."

Furthermore, the term has terrific functional potential, as it clearly suggests the course of action needed to counteract the pressure: expand the walls of the container or change the temperature. Perhaps that's why we favor open spaces and vast panoramas, and why psychologists tell us to take trips when we're under stress. The next time office tension closes in on you, you can say, "I'm boyling up under all this pressure. If Joe calls, tell him I drove down to the beach to cool my thermometer."

The metaffect has even more constructive possibilities. For example, imagine a room filled with nervous colleagues pacing the floor, chomping on pencils, and gulping down antacid tablets. Your boss, having been up for thirty-six hours trying to solve the problem, is gazing blankly into space. Suddenly, you remember this metaffect. You stand up and declare, "Let's look at this scientifically. Boyle's Law states that pressure goes up when the size of the container is reduced and the temperature is constant, right? Well, I say, let's push back the walls of the container—expand our horizons, broaden our perspective, and cool things down by stopping all the arguing. Our mistakes may have gotten us into this mess, but Boyle's Law can get us out of it."

Brownian Motion

In an old movie whose title I can't recall, the camera is stationed on the ceiling of New York's Grand Central Station. Looking down, we see hundreds of speck-sized bodies swarming about in random patterns. That is the kind of image the Scottish botanist Robert Brown must have seen through his microscope in 1827 as he studied grains of pollen suspended in water. Brown, an explorer, curator of the British Museum, and discoverer of the cell nucleus, made an astonishing discovery: the particles, about one four-thousandth of an inch long, moved in a kind of ceaseless, trembling, irregular zigzag. The phenomenon came to be called *Brownian Movement* or *Brownian Motion*.

Brown repeated the experiment with pollen from a number of different plants. It turned out that all of the granules, if small enough, showed the same kind of motion when suspended in water. Subsequently, Brown found that the same was true of small particles of inorganic substances as well. In fact, it was true of all colloidal suspensions—mixtures in which one substance is divided into minute particles and dispersed throughout a second substance, whether solid-in-liquid, liquid-in-liquid, gas-in-liquid, solid-in-gas, or liquid-in-gas. In the words of Albert Einstein, who would, eighty years later, work out a mathematical formulation to explain Brownian Motion, "The amazing thing is the apparently eternal character of the motion. . . . The existence of a never diminishing motion seems contrary to all experience."

Ultimately, the analysis of Brownian Motion contributed to the now-familiar notion that gases and liquids are composed of a large number of extremely small units called molecules. It turns out that the solid particles Brown observed were being bombarded by the smaller invisible particles that comprised the water in which they were suspended. The motion of the observable particles is so bizarre because their bombardment is constant, irregular, and haphazard.

As a metaffect, Brownian Motion is a perfect way to describe today's urban congestion. No doubt you've felt like a Brownian particle at times, when your body was being buffeted about in a large, bustling crowd of strangers—at Times Square on New Year's Eve, a commuter station at rush hour, a parade or rally when rain begins to fall, or a rock concert where seating is first come, first served.

The next time you're in such a situation, you can perhaps take comfort in the notion that, as with Brownian Motion, there might be some rational explanation for what you are going through or an orderly pattern you simply can't perceive from the middle of the chaos. If your companions are aggravated by the conditions, you can say, "Look at it this way. We're all just tiny particles in a colloidal suspension in Brownian Motion." It may not be much of a consolation, but your analogy might take their minds off their discomfort.

Brownian Motion also aptly describes certain mental conditions. For example, if you've ever tried to accomplish anything slightly out of the ordinary at a Motor Vehicle Bureau, or registered for classes at a large university, or been shuffled from one faceless bureaucrat to another at city hall, you know what it feels like to have your mind jostled around like a Brownian particle. The next time you run up against such intractable conditions, you will have a fresher and more provocative alternative to the overused "I feel like a character in a Kafka novel." You will be able to say, "This is absurd. I refuse to be treated like some grain of pollen in Brownian Motion." That should get their attention.

The metaffect is also a colorful way to describe the state of your brain when an excess of demands have it hopping around from one thought to another in a zigzag, aimless fashion. Under such confused conditions you might want to take a break, so just tell everyone, "Excuse me, I have to get my bearings. My brain cells are kicking around like Brownian particles, and you know what that means." (They may not, of course, but they'll be terribly impressed.)

Brownian Motion also suggests that an object can appear to be self-propelled when, in fact, its environment is causing it to move. The next time you think you have made up your mind on some issue all on your own, you might remember Robert Brown's petrie dish and ask yourself whether the currents of your culture might not be more responsible for where you are and how you are moving than your own internally generated ideas. None of us is beyond being moved by unseen forces. The Brownian tide of the social *Zeitgeist* can storm-toss and drown even expert swimmers.

If the metaffect catches on, perhaps it will one day become common parlance. Radio traffic reports might contain lines like "It's been pure Brownian Motion out there ever since the ten-wheeler jackknifed at First and Main." Perhaps travel agents will say, "If you'd like a real Brownian experience, I suggest you get to Pamplona the day of the running of the bulls." Coffee cans will contain the warning "Caution: when used in excess, product causes Brownian Motion of the nerve cells." And parents will warn their kids, "I don't want you anywhere near that rally. It's going to be Brownian hell down there."

The Butterfly Effect

On December 29, 1979, Edward Lorenz, a research meteorologist at MIT, gave a speech to the American Association for the Advancement of Science titled "Predictability: Does the Flap of a Butterfly's Wings in Brazil Set Off a Tornado in Texas?" Lorenz' image gave the name to a principle that has since become a central precept of a new branch of science called Chaos Theory. Technically, the *Butterfly Effect* is defined as "sensitive dependence on initial conditions." It means, essentially, that small changes can become magnified over the course of a subsequent chain of events and culminate in a major, large-scale happening.

As author James Gleick explains in his book *Chaos: Making a New Science,* "In systems like the weather, sensitive dependence on initial conditions was an inescapable consequence of the way small scales intertwined with large." In other words, a minor event like the flapping of a butterfly's wings could conceivably alter wind currents sufficiently to eventually impact weather conditions a few thousand miles away. Or, as the familiar verse puts it, "For want of a nail, the shoe was lost; for want of a shoe, the horse was lost; for want of a horse, the

rider was lost; for want of a rider, the battle was lost; for want of a battle, the kingdom was lost."

Like many pivotal concepts in science, the Butterfly Effect was discovered by accident. In 1960, on a primitive computer, Lorenz created a method of mathematically modeling climatic conditions. He was hoping to find a way to analyze complex, never-repeating weather patterns so as to make possible the old dream of accurate long-range prediction. Lorenz hoped to identify the laws governing meteorology with such precision that, by calculating the state of the system at one moment in time, one would be able to predict its condition at any point in the future. This was not to be, thanks to the Butterfly Effect.

According to Gleick's book, to save time on a particular calculation, Lorenz one day entered into his computer a rounded-off figure, .506, instead of the more complete number, .506127, which he had used in an earlier trial. He assumed that the change in value of less than 1 one-thousandth would be inconsequential; it was not. When his simulation of weather conditions came out markedly different from the initial run-through of the same data, Lorenz realized that, in Gleick's words, "something was philosophically out of joint . . . he decided that long-range weather forecasting must be doomed." The seemingly trivial numerical alteration was the equivalent of the puff of wind created by a butterfly's wings, and yet it had produced a tremendous difference in the predicted outcome.

In the long run, the kind of computer modeling that Lorenz originated did, in fact, make weather prediction dramatically more precise, but only for a few days' duration. After that, the calculations seem to be useless because of the Butterfly Effect. A small change at any point can spark a chain of events that sets weather conditions rolling in an entirely different direction that is impossible to predict. As Gleick puts it, "Errors and uncertainties multiply, cascading upward through a chain of turbulent features, from dust devils and squalls up to continent-size eddies that only satellites can see."

Among the many implications of the Butterfly Effect is this: in many instances, predicting the future with absolute accuracy is virtually impossible. Theoretically, the consequences of any minor error in measurement, or any overlooked variable, will magnify as it moves through the system, gathering momentum like water down a series of falls, until the result at the end of the line is far more powerful than the initial trickle could possibly have suggested. Fittingly, Edward Lorenz' attempt at a shortcut (leaving out a few decimal places) became an example of the principle itself; his discovery led to a chain of events that resulted in the new science of chaos.

The Butterfly Effect can be applied metaffectively to a variety of everyday matters where small events generate large, unforeseen repercussions. In the early stages of a project, for example, it can drive home the importance of the maxim "Well begun is half done." The smart executive thus might advise his colleagues, "Remember the Butterfly Effect; even the smallest individual actions can have an enormous effect on large systems. Any tiny error, any minor miscalculation, any momentary lapse in concentration or judgment can lead to disastrous consequences down the road."

Tragically, we have seen this happen already: in the defective "O" rings on the Challenger, which doomed the space shuttle and the astronauts aboard, and in the error in a foundry in 1971, which caused a microscopic flaw in the composition of titanium, which in turn led to a crack in a small engine part, which caused the fatal crash of a passenger jet in Sioux City, Iowa, in 1989.

In a more positive vein, business people can use the metaffect to motivate employees. Try this on your new trainees: "No one in this company is insignificant. No one's ideas are too small to be aired. We believe that any little insight, a casual remark, a minor compliment, an encouraging gesture, a minor improvement on some trivial operation, a change of words in giving instructions—any of these can create a Butterfly Effect and make a big difference in the future of our venture."

The metaffect is also an encouraging reminder that any one of us, acting in the service of a cherished principle, can make a difference, perhaps altering the course of events in our communities. The next time you think that taking arms against a sea of troubles would not be worth the bother, remember the impact of a simple flap of a butterfly's wings. If you encounter a naysayer, instead of reciting the old saw about "for want of a nail," you can invoke a new, recondite branch of science: "You think I'm wasting my time lobbying for a recycling program? Well, let me tell you about the Butterfly Effect."

The metaffect has other, more metaphysical, implications too. Despite its name, Chaos Theory does not view the universe as random but as subject to a high level of mathematical order.

In the words of Douglas Hofstadter, author of *Gödel, Escher, Bach,* "It turns out that an eerie type of chaos can lurk just behind a facade of order—and yet, deep inside the chaos lurks an even eerier type of order." It is comforting to know that there might be a method to the madness around us, that the natural forces impinging on us are not as random as they seem.

This sense of the metaffect can be especially useful when life becomes turbulent, when travesties and tragedies are heaped upon you with no apparent rhyme or reason and you can't make sense of anything. Maybe that cold you can't shake began when someone sneezed in Hong Kong. Maybe the car accident you just had was set in motion by a little old lady in Pasadena who ran out of gas. Maybe today's international crisis had its roots in the boudoir of some unknown woman the night before. Like the Indian concept of *karma,* the Butterfly Effect suggests that cause-and-effect laws are applicable in the universe even if the pattern is indecipherable and the precise causes of our predicaments, rooted far away in time and space, are ultimately unfathomable.

The Butterfly Effect ought to make us more mindful of our actions. If a wave of a hand or a stone thrown over a precipice might change the weather on another continent, imagine the impact you can have with a careless word or a lapse in manners: "I know that guy cut you off, but I wish you hadn't sworn at him. I'm sure you'll cause a Butterfly Effect. You piss him off, so then he gives the finger to some guy who tailgates him, and that guy gets home and yells at his wife, and the wife gets cross with the kids, so the kids go out to play and ridicule their friends, and the friends go home and aggravate their baby-sitter, so the baby-sitter breaks up with her boyfriend, and he goes out and gets drunk and drives home. . . ."

Perhaps it's more uplifting to gaze up at the dark dome of night and wonder if, by lighting a match, you can have an impact on the future of a star. Or to contemplate whether the Butterfly Effect might not validate the old homily "Smile and the whole world smiles with you."

Capgras' Syndrome

Did you ever look at a person with whom you have a close relationship—a spouse, a parent, a sibling—and suddenly have the thought "Who *is* this person?" For a brief, disquieting moment, it's as if you had never laid eyes on him or her before. Well, take that unusual experience to the extreme and you might be able to imagine what it's like to suffer from *Capgras' Syndrome.*

Someone afflicted with this disorder comes to believe that a familiar person, usually a close relative, has been replaced by an impostor who has assumed the exact appearance of the supplanted party. A rare pathological condition that occurs most often in schizophrenics, Capgras' Syndrome also appears in certain cases of organic disease of the brain.

The disorder was first described by two French physicians, Capgras and Reboul-Lachaux, in 1923 (why Reboul-Lachaux's name was denied by history I do not know). They called the disorder *L'illusion des sosies,* a term derived from a Greek myth in which Zeus impersonated Amphitryon in order to seduce that warrior's wife. To facilitate his deception, Zeus persuaded Mercury to assume the form of Amphitryon's servant, Socies. The mistaken identity that resulted gave rise to the name. (Perhaps, had the diagnosis been made after 1956, the doctors might have given it a more contemporary twist and called it "Invasion of the Body Snatchers Syndrome," after the horror-movie classic in which the residents of a small town are replaced one by one by clones hatched from alien pods.)

Capgras' Syndrome is a fixed delusional belief marked by hostility toward the "impostor" and normal feelings of affection for the "real" person, whom the patient thinks has been replaced. It is easy to see how a troubled mind might create such an illusion in order to compensate for ambivalent feelings. By inventing an impostor, the person is absolved of the guilt he would otherwise feel for having strong hostility toward a loved one.

Of what use to the rest of us is a term about a pathological condition? Think of it as a metaphor for seeing any familiar person in an entirely new light. The term could, for example, serve as a clever way of expressing astonishment when someone defies your expectations. Suppose one of your employees, whose intelligence you considered ordinary at best, suddenly presents you with a brilliant business plan. In requesting a raise for her, you might say, "Either I have Capgras' Syndrome or she's not what I thought she was."

Of course, it might work in the opposite direction, as when a spouse or lover or friend suddenly reveals a venal or selfish streak you had never before seen: "Dear, I hope I have Capgras' Syndrome, because you're certainly not the man I married."

Then there are those occasions when people express surprise at something you do: "Why are you looking at me like that? Do you have Capgras' Syndrome or something? I've *always* been a good dancer."

Women reentering the work force can use the metaffect when their families express skepticism about their qualifications: "Listen up, you guys. You've seen me run this house, manage the finances, repair gadgets, nurse illnesses, serve as chauffeur, answering service, and guidance counselor, and you think I'm incapable of working in the so-called real world? What is this, an epidemic of Capgras' Syndrome? Oh, you've never heard of it, eh? I guess I have to be a teacher also."

Cepheid Variables

In the eighteenth century, astronomers discovered that a star in the constellation Cepheus would brighten and dim, brighten and dim, in cycles of 5.3 days. They named this star of fluctuating luminosity Delta Cephei. Subsequently, other such stars were discovered, all yellow "supergiants" whose periods from brightest to dimmest (caused by actual physical pulsations that alter their temperature and size) ranged from less than a day to about two months. They were named *Cepheid Variables* (pronounced *see*-fee-id).

This category of stars turned out to have great significance in the evolution of astronomy. The period of a Cepheid Variable depends on its intrinsic brightness, or "absolute magnitude"—the brighter the star, the longer its cycle. By measuring a Cepheid's period, astronomers can determine its absolute magnitude or true brightness. Then, by comparing its true brightness to how bright it appears to us, they can calculate its distance from earth. Because of this property, Cepheids are invaluable in estimating the distances between stars and galaxies. They hence came to be called "the yardsticks of the universe." The extra measure of accuracy that Cepheid Variables provided enabled astronomers to realize that the universe is twice as vast, and therefore much older, than was previously thought.

As a metaffect, the term might signify a person or phenomenon whose brightness fluctuates. Did you ever feel that your personal star shines brilliantly, only to dim, then flash again, then fade, perhaps not with the regularity of a Delta Cephei but with disconcerting frequency nonetheless? We are, after all, subject to fluctuations in energy due to various biorhythms and physiological processes such as the rise and fall of blood-sugar levels. If you are sensitive to your own rhythms, you might find occasion to say, "Four o'clock? Can we make it ten A.M. instead? I want to shine at that meeting, and I'm a Cepheid Variable—I'm totally luminous first thing in the morning, but by mid-afternoon I start to fade out."

If you've ever been involved with a Cepheid personality—particularly one whose range from the brightest to the dimmest is extreme—you know how disconcerting they can be. You can now tell that person, "Please see a doctor, honey, your mood swings are driving me crazy. You're a Cepheid Variable and you need professional help."

The metaffect can also be applied to those who flash into the public eye with incandescent brilliance only to fade from view, rock stars and movie stars being the most obvious examples. Performers like Michael Jackson and the Rolling Stones shine and dim with the regularity of a Cepheid Variable, sparkling with a new album and a blockbuster concert tour, then fading into relative obscurity. Marlon Brando, Al Pacino, and other talents of luminous absolute magnitude shine in the Hollywood heavens, then disappear from view while their agents and managers await their return like astronomers anticipating Halley's Comet. Greta Garbo might be the ultimate Cepheid Variable. She shone so brightly that she's still talked about fifty years after retreating into voluntary anonymity; articles and videotapes serve to keep her periodically, albeit dimly, in view.

Athletes who earn the label "streak player" are metaffective

Cepheid Variables. Their skills fluctuate radically in periods of brief duration: they perform with consummate brilliance for a spell, then go into hellacious slumps, then streak again like shooting stars, only to fade into another slump, and so forth. You might suggest, "Moose is starting to dim again. Maybe we should hire a coach who specializes in Cepheid Variables."

Of course, the term can be applied to non-public figures as well: "Say, whatever happened to Bernie? He was the Golden Boy around here for a while, but then he sort of faded into oblivion."

"Oh, Bernie was fired. He went to work for Acme. Set a sales record his first month there, then laid a supergiant egg. Now he's pounding the pavement. Don't worry, he'll shine again. Bernie's one of those Cepheid Variables."

Parents of moody kids might say, "I don't know what to do about Junior. He's like the kid in the nursery rhyme—when he's good he's very good, but when he's bad he's horrid. I'm afraid we have a Cepheid Variable on our hands."

Fussy diners might use the metaffect this way: "They should rename this restaurant 'The Cepheid Variable.' Some nights their food is out of this world, but other times it ought to be dumped into a black hole."

About inconsistent service persons, one might complain, "My hairdresser is a genius, but she's as erratic as a Cepheid Variable. She can make you look like a movie star or a witch, depending on the phase she's in."

The Chappaquidick Theorem

The infamous incident in 1969 that seems to have permanently barred Edward M. Kennedy from the White House has given us a metaffect with great potential. The body of Mary Jo Kopechne was found dead in a car that Senator Kennedy had driven off the Chappaquidick bridge on Martha's Vineyard late the previous night. The resulting scandal made for titillating coffee-break chatter, because Kennedy was married and Ms. Kopechne was a young, single, attractive member of his staff. But what permanently tainted Kennedy's career was his failure to report the incident until the next morning. Because of that lapse, the public and press become convinced that the Senator had committed a serious indiscretion. Had he gone straight to the police and reported the incident, he might have been given the benefit of the doubt.

Based on Kennedy's experience, James Doyle, the public-affairs spokesman for Archibald Cox, Special Prosecutor in the Watergate trials, coined the term *Chappaquidick Theorem,* which has been explained as follows by historian Theodore H. White: "There is no good time for a political figure to tell bad news except right away. If there is bad news, devoted advisers will tell the principal to wait until tomorrow, or wait until next month when the bad news can be covered with a good headline. But all such well-meaning advice is wrong: the longer a political leader waits to put forth his bad news, the worse will be its effect."

According to White, all the events in Nixon's ill-fated White House after February 1973 can be attributed to the President's refusal to accept the Chappaquidick Theorem. The infamous White House tapes indicate that Nixon conceived of his problem as a matter of high-stakes public relations. His advisers chose what they called the "hangout route," a strategy in which they would reveal, in fragments and distortions, only what was safe to tell about Watergate lest the press force the whole truth out into the open.

In the tapes of March 22, the day after he ordered the payment of $75,000 in hush money to E. Howard Hunt, Nixon told Attorney General John Mitchell, "I don't give a [expletive deleted] what happens. I want you all to stonewall it, let them plead the Fifth Amendment, cover-up or anything else, if it'll save it—save the plan." For Nixon, of course, it saved nothing. As Sam Ervin, the chairman of the Senate committee investigating Watergate, was to say, quoting Sir Walter Scott, "Oh, what a tangled web we weave, when first we practice to deceive."

What applies to political leaders whose every decision is scrutinized by a carnivorous press might not apply to you and me in our relatively anonymous dealings; nevertheless, the Chappaquidick Theorem is a worthy metaffect. When faced with an unpleasant situation in which you can tell the full truth, cover it up, or hope it will all go away, you can remind yourself of Ted Kennedy and Richard Nixon and invoke the principle.

Suppose you made a damaging mistake at work. Do you acknowledge your culpability or hope no one will notice? If you clam up, what do you do later when your error produces consequences and inquisitive noses start sniffing around for the cause? You can admit to a lesser, more palatable offense in hope that the explanation will shut the door on further inquiries (as when politicians say they committed an "error of judgment," not a violation of law or ethics), or you can boldly and courageously fess up in hopes of earning the compassion and respect that often accompanies such candor. If your colleagues argue against total honesty, your response might be, "No, according to the Chappaquidick Theorem, the longer I wait, the worse it is likely to be."

The metaffect can be applied to bad news of a trivial sort as well as major confessions: you crack your wife's favorite vase; you burn your husband's best shirt; you forget to tell your daughter that Harry Hunk called. Do you delay reporting the mishap, hoping no one will notice, or wait for a plausible excuse to flash into mind, or search for some ideal truth-telling moment? The Chappaquidick Theorem suggests you would do well to tell the truth expeditiously.

I recently learned that lesson when I received my second traffic ticket in as many months. I considered concealing the incident in the hope that it would never come to my wife's attention since she teases me unmercifully about my driving style. But, recalling the Chappaquidick Theorem, I decided to confess immediately, with appropriate contrition, rather than risk the added onus of a bungled cover-up. My wife's considerate refusal to gloat indicates that I made the right choice.

Verification of the theorem's efficacy in everyday life is usually just a flick of the dial away. Without knowing the name for it, comedy writers have been weaving screwball plots around the Chappaquidick Theorem ever since Lucille Ball tried unsuccessfully to conceal wacky deeds from Ricky. Perhaps Richard Nixon, who was Dwight Eisenhower's Vice President at the time, was too busy to watch "I Love Lucy."

The Cocktail Party Effect

You are at a cocktail party and someone is chewing your ear with a story you couldn't care less about. You nod politely, working your face into an expression of profound interest, while paying just enough attention to assure that you don't smile or frown or nod at an inappropriate time. Meanwhile, a cacophony of party sounds impinges on your ears; a kaleidoscope of forms and colors enters and leaves your vision; you are jostled and bumped by dancing couples; you feed your taste buds with tangy snacks and sweet libations. And yet, with all this input, you are still able to zero in on a conversation ten feet away—the one involving a certain someone you wish to meet, or which just might provide you with some advantageous gossip. You can hear the words and comprehend their meaning despite the interference of sounds and sights much closer to you.

This is what psychologists call the *Cocktail Party Effect*: the rejection of unwanted messages by the senses in favor of more pertinent or interesting information. Because our nervous systems are subjected to much more stimulation than we can possibly use, nature provided our brains with an extremely useful trait—the ability to be conscious of only a limited amount of information at any given moment. Exactly how we manage to block, or at least weaken, unwanted input is by and large a mystery that has intrigued the best minds in science since the days of William James at the turn of the century. Apparently, a number of factors aid in the selection process.

In the case of hearing, which is the principle domain of the Cocktail Party Effect, a major component of the filtering is "binaural hearing," the process by which we use both ears to locate the direction of sound sources by analyzing differences in phase or amplitude. Other factors play a role as well: where the speakers are located in space, differences in voice timbre, the sex of the speaker, the quality of the voice, the emotional content of the message, and so forth.

The next time you are in a crowd, notice how dialogue that doesn't interest you turns into an indecipherable hum. Compare that to how well you can monitor an equally faint conversation if you hear your own name mentioned. Notice how you can be distracted by a voice that stands out in the cacophony because it is unusually high-pitched or strident or because the speaker uses foul language, or speaks in an unusual accent, or is talking about something so titillating it breaks right through to your brain like the commercial jingles you try to tune out only to find yourself humming them in the shower.

In essence, we have in this concept a metaffect about the selectivity of perception. The next time you have a squabble with your spouse or a business associate—one of those infuriating debates in which the other person seems to have been on another planet when you presented your astute and impeccably

reasoned argument—you can blame the other party's lapse on the convenient use of the Cocktail Party Effect. Furthermore, as with most terms that come from respected sources like psychology or medicine, the metaffect will be more convincing and less threatening, and it will disarm your opponent far more effectively than the equivalent vernacular. Think of the difference between "I believe you tuned out because of the Cocktail Party Effect" and "You're not listening to a goddamn word I say!"

By extension, the term is also a perfect way to describe those instances when you and a companion, on your way home from an event, discover that your perceptions of what took place and your conclusions about the personalities in attendance are poles apart. You think the guy in the red tie was a pompous jerk; your companion thinks he was a charming raconteur. You loved it when the band played "Hey Jude"; your friend says they never played the song. You think the after-dinner speaker was a right-wing fascist; your partner thinks he was a flaming liberal. Now, instead of descending into an argument that is bound to end in futility (or cause a Boomerang Effect), you can simply sigh, "It must be the Cocktail Party Effect. You tuned out what I tuned in."

The Complementarity Principle

A particle is, by definition, a solid object, a piece of something. A wave is *not* a solid object; it is an oscillation in a uniform medium, like water or air. On the surface, it would seem that nothing could be both a particle and a wave. But physicists in the early part of this century found out otherwise. They discovered that light is made up of particles called photons, yet it also behaves like a wave. If a scientist wants to demonstrate the particle properties of light, he can; if he wants to demonstrate the wave properties of light, again he can. This paradox blew the collective mind of physics.

Niels Bohr set the matter straight with his *Complementarity Priniciple*. A towering figure in modern science, Bohr was director of the Institute of Theoretical Physics in Copenhagen, Denmark, and the recipient of a Nobel Prize in 1922. To Bohr, it was meaningless to argue over whether light is really a particle or a wave, because it is both. The wave and the particle are not the defining properties of light, as such, but in fact properties of the way we interact with light.

Bohr's Complementarity Principle suggests that the material world is fraught with paradox. We can't imagine something being a wave and particle at the same time, yet that is the case. And it turns out to be true not only of light, but of all the elementary particles that make up matter; in a laboratory, they can behave like waves and also like particles. Therefore, it is true of everything. Properties that seem to be mutually exclusive actually coexist as essential complements of one another.

Bohr's principle forces upon us a certain flexibility of mind, particularly if we apply the concept metaffectively. In many ways, human affairs are mirrors of the microscopic world that physicists study (as below, so above). People are fraught with paradox, and living gracefully with that essential truth might well be a measure of maturity. Like light, we are made up of conflicting properties and seemingly incongruous traits. We, too, behave disconcertingly, with our myriad inconsistencies and mysterious contradictions. We are by nature as paradoxical as the elementary particle-waves that make up our very atoms—good and bad, generous and selfish, stupid and smart, childish and mature, beautiful and ugly, and so on. And, as with light observed by a physicist, people often can be whatever we want them to be.

Romance is a fertile arena for this metaffect. For example, you probably know any number of women who have said, "I don't know what to make of this guy. He's kind and he's sweet. But he can also be self-centered and inconsiderate. He's gentle, but he's also abusive. He's exciting, but he's also a bore. I love him and I hate him."

Now, after nodding sympathetically, you can reply, "So, what else is new? That's life. That's human nature. That's the Complementarity Principle. You have to accept the paradox and do what you can to bring out the side you like."

Many expressions have become clichés because they reflect conditions of complementarity: "You seem so near, yet so far away." "It feels like only yesterday, but then again it feels like it's been forever." "It seems the more things change, the more they stay the same." "Is the glass half full or half empty?" Now, thanks to Niels Bohr, you know that such perceptions are not necessarily contradictions; they simply reflect an essential property of life on earth.

As a metaffect, the term also has rich metaphysical and spiritual connotations. Mystics of all traditions have perceived of existence as eternally changing yet never-changing, interminably moving yet still, relentlessly relative yet absolute. In the Orient, this primal complementarity has long been recognized, as Niels Bohr discovered when he visited China in 1937. So impressed was he by the Taoist notion that the universe is composed of archetypal opposites—the yielding, receptive, intuitive, female *yin* and the dynamic, forceful, rational, masculine *yang*—that he chose its now-familiar symbol, the *T'ai-chi T'u*, for his coat of arms when he was knighted by Denmark. The heraldic inscription he selected was *Contraria sunt complementa*, "opposites are complementary."

It's one we would all do well to emblazon on the shields of our psyches. Recalling the Complementarity Principle might soothe your troubled soul and help you get your bearings when life seems overwhelmingly paradoxical.

The Coolidge Effect

After an orgasmic sexual experience, how long, or how soon, is it before a male is ready to have another go at it?

This question is of interest not only to macho raconteurs in saloons and concerned females in salons, but to scientists who research sexual behavior. In fact, those who focus their studies on animals have established norms for male recovery time, which vary, of course, from one species to another, rats being different from roosters, which are different from rams. The pattern they've discovered goes like this: Get a male alone with a female in heat and copulation will occur rather quickly. Then, after the initial ejaculation, the male will refrain for a predictable amount of time before mounting again. After another decent interval, a third coupling will occur, then a fourth and a fifth, and so on until the male is exhausted.

The recovery time will be longer with each successive ejaculation. That is, between the second and third copulations, a longer interval will elapse than between the first and second, and the interval between the third and fourth will be even longer than that—the male pauses longer and longer each time.

I can't imagine that this comes as a surprise to humans of either sex. But here is the interesting part: if, after any of the series of trysts, you remove the female and replace her with a new sex partner, it's back to square one in terms of recovery time for the male. To our eyes, one female monkey may look just like any other, as do hens, ewes, and mares. But to the male of the species, whose sexual response is finely tuned to the olfactory sense, the difference can be profoundly invigorating. When a new female enters the scene, the male's interest perks up; he is ready to pounce a lot faster than he would be if the first gal were still in the cage.

Even after the male has reached total exhaustion, if a new female sashays into the boudoir, his recovery time might be as rapid as it was after the very first encounter. And, if you keep introducing new females, the male will continue his potent performance for a remarkably long period of time. This is called the *Coolidge Effect.*

Was the effect named after a curious researcher name Coolidge? Or after an especially lecherous experimental subject? Neither. It was named after the thirtieth President of the United States, Calvin Coolidge, the austere New England conservative whose nickname was "Silent Cal" and whose personal demeanor was so sour as to inspire Alice Roosevelt Longworth to remark, "He was weaned on a pickle." The reason for the name is contained in the following story, which may be apocryphal but *ought* to be true if it is not.

It seems that Silent Cal was visiting a government farm with his wife, the former Grace A. Goodhue, who was renowned for her poise and charm. The large number of chicks and the high production of eggs on the farm prompted Mrs. Coolidge to remark that all the fecundity must require prodigious effort by the roosters. The farmer replied, proudly, that indeed the roosters performed their duties dozens of times a day. "You might point that out to Mr. Coolidge," the First Lady reportedly said.

Cal may have been the silent type, but he was evidently no prude. He, in turn, asked the farmer if each hard-working rooster had to service the same hen each time. No, said the farmer, variety was the spice of a rooster's life. Replied the President, "You might point that out to Mrs. Coolidge."

While opinions vary as to the efficacy of applying the results of animal studies to human beings, the value of adding this term to one's vocabulary will be instantly obvious, particularly to a man who might find it a convenient biological explanation for certain behavior: "I'm sorry, honey, I just can't help it. It's that damned Coolidge Effect again." (We'll know the term has caught on when women start forming Coolidge Effect support groups.)

On the other hand, women might find it useful to inform their men, at the appropriate moment, that human females are not as tolerant as their bestial sisters. Turnabout being fair play among humans if not among monkeys and rats, they might suggest that women are not prohibited by instinct from engaging in the same behavior as men: "Shape up, Joe, or you'll find yourself on the wrong side of the Coolidge Effect. Variety can spice up the goose's life as well as the gander's."

Women might also keep in mind something that many have discovered on their own, and that studies confirm, at least in animals: the male's vigor can be renewed even when the original female sticks around if stimuli such as appearance or scent are altered. I can hear the bedroom conversation now:

"Wow! Where did you get that incredible perfume?"

"Do you like it? It's Eau de Calvin, an antidote to the Coolidge Effect."

"Gee, I guess I'm not that tired after all."

The Coolidge Effect can also be used in a broader metaffective context for the renewal of vigor, in either gender, due to freshness and variety. For example, suppose you find it more and more difficult at work to summon the energy to do the same tedious task day after day. It takes you longer and longer to get the same amount of work done and longer and longer to get back to it after each break. You might even be on the brink of burnout, the equivalent of sexual exhaustion. Then, something new comes along: a new task, a new wrinkle on the old job, a new location in which to perform the work, or a new colleague with whom to do it. Your interest and your energy suddenly perk up, and you get back to the job immediately after each interruption: "It's incredible. As soon as we moved our offices the Coolidge Effect kicked in, and I'm really jazzed about my work." Or, "I've decided not to quit after all. My supervisor gave me a new assignment and I feel coolidged already."

If you're a manager or supervisor, the metaffect can become an important motivational tool: "Okay, it's time to shake things up around here. This place needs the Coolidge Effect." Then you can rearrange assignments, alter the environment, switch partners, or whatever. And when you win an award for the fecundity and potency of your department's output, you can say in your acceptance speech, "I owe it all to Calvin Coolidge," and wow the audience with a stimulating presidential anecdote.

In your personal life, you might intentionally activate the Coolidge Effect to energize a task that threatens to become redundant, monotonous, or tiresome. For example, studies show that nearly half of all people who take up an exercise program drop out after six months. Chances are, a principal reason is boredom. So, why not coolidge your exercise regimen by switching from, say, jogging to bicycling to swimming to an aerobics class, where you just might meet someone with sex appeal and . . . a double Coolidge Effect!

The Cooling-Off Principle

For as far back as history records, there have always been men who fought wars and others who worked diligently to put an end to them. The peace movements of modern times have been unique in that they have constructed careful philosophical arguments against *all* war. Such antiwar doctrines were built on two legs: pacifist philosophies, which argued variously that war was destructive, unnecessary, economically wasteful, or a violation of Judeo-Christian tenets; and constructive approaches that called for rational solutions to the causes of war and machinery for resolving conflicts.

Concerning the latter, peace activists devised specific methods that they hoped governments would accept and employ: arbitration, conciliation, mediation, inquiry, and the use of diplomacy. The hope for each of these was that a nonpartisan third party could propose suitable solutions for the problems that threatened war between two nations.

Between 1870 and 1914, antiwar efforts centered on getting nations to agree to broad treaty provisions, under which they would submit all their differences to arbitration. The weakness of this approach became clear as tensions built toward the conflagration of World War I. In spite of a patchwork of treaties, not a single European government suggested that the nettlesome issues of the day be resolved by arbitration. While they did submit to arbitration trivial matters such as legal misunderstandings and treaty interpretations, no country would risk having an arbiter decide anything involving its vital interests.

Pacifists then came up with another formula: conciliation. Issues that were not submitted to arbitration could be referred to a third party, which would make specific, but nonbinding, recommendations. In the early twentieth century, this approach gained support when it was strengthened by the *Cooling-Off Principle,* which was included in several treaties. Under this principle, hostilities were postponed while a commission worked toward conciliation. Then, after the commission rendered its decision, an additional moratorium on warfare was required, usually covering a period of six months.

The Cooling-Off Principle was rooted in the assumption

that wars begin in moments of heated passion. Advocates such as Secretary of State William Jennings Bryan believed that, if nations delayed hostilities and explored their problems calmly and rationally, tempers were bound to cool and armed struggle would not erupt. However, in practice, the prohibition against fighting had no teeth whatsoever. Thus, despite the inclusion of the Cooling-Off Principle, conciliation policies failed to avert World War I.

In the end, the Cooling-Off Principle did not work for nations, but it can serve as a useful metaffect for interpersonal conflicts. Recommending the Cooling-Off Principle for ordinary discord may sound like some pop-psych equivalent of an old wives' tale, but that does not lessen its efficacy. After all, distance—in time or space or both—from volatile events can reduce emotional tension, allowing hostile parties to contemplate the situation more rationally. Knowing the name of the concept and its long and notable history in international diplomacy may invest you with an aura of authority, encouraging those who are quick on the trigger to take you seriously.

Consider the following conversation between rival businessmen:

"Look, Max, let's agree not to do anything rash for two weeks, so that . . . "

"Drop dead, I'm suing you today!"

"Listen, there's an honorable precedent called the Cooling-Off Principle. Here's my suggestion. . . ."

Parents might intervene when their kids are squabbling: "Listen up, brats, I'm imposing the Cooling-Off Principle. I want each of you to take five minutes alone in your room before you say another word."

Of course, there will be occasions when you have to convince even yourself that the principle is worth the effort. The next time you pick up the phone to tell a coworker exactly what you think about his taking credit for your idea, or grab the handle on your car door ready to pounce on the guy who cut you off, or when strangulation strikes you as a more effective solution to marital strife than discussion, just think of the Cooling-Off Principle. Declare a moratorium on hostilities for a set period of time. Wars between nations may not start in moments of passion, but regrettable clashes between individuals surely do (see the Babinski Reflex).

As a metaffect, the concept might be used not just for interpersonal disputes, but internally. When you are overheated by emotion—particularly when you are furious at yourself for a blunder you made or an indignity you foisted on yourself—you are prone to regrettable actions. Applying a psychic ice pack might spare you further suffering, perhaps even prevent you from waging war on yourself through some self-destructive behavior: "Whew! Good thing my left brain stepped in with the Cooling-Off Principle. My right brain was in attack mode."

The Coriolis Effect

If you start at the center of a spinning carousel and walk toward a point on the outer edge, the ground beneath your feet will move faster and faster as you progress. If the carousel is spinning counterclockwise, you will feel yourself veering clockwise. Reversing your path, if you begin at the edge and move toward the center, you will start out walking rapidly, but the ground under you will move slower and slower and you will begin to feel pulled, again clockwise. If you follow both paths in succession, starting near the center and moving toward the outer edge, then going back toward the center, you will find that your path is roughly circular.

The reason for all this is simple: the interior of a spinning object moves more slowly then the edges because it has a shorter distance to travel in the same amount of time. A point on the outer rim has to traverse a large circle, while a point in the center has to mark only a small one.

Since earth is a rotating sphere, the principle holds true for the entire planet. The distance traveled in one complete rotation is obviously far greater at the equator than traveled at a latitude such as New York's, and that distance is far greater than one traveled at still higher latitudes, such as that of Alaska. Hence, at the equator, a body whirls at nearly 1,670 kilometers an hour, while in New York its speed is 1,280 and in southern Alaska, 800. At the North Pole an object would slowly spin at a rate of one rotation per day.

As with a person walking across a carousel, something moving north or south on earth, or above it—say, an ocean current or a wind or a rocket—will have its course altered, because different parts of the earth move at different rates of speed. Since the planet rotates from west to east and spins most rapidly at the equator, an object traveling from one of the poles toward the equator tends to fall behind and veer to the west. Something moving toward either pole *from* the equator will veer eastward. This sideways drift is called the *Coriolis Effect,* after the French physicist Gaspard del Coriolis, who discovered the phenomenon in 1835.

Because our legs and automobiles move too slowly for the spin of earth to matter a lot, we are generally unaware of the Coriolis Effect. But meteorologists, aeronautical engineers, and rocket scientists are very much aware of it, since the phenomenon creates the trade winds, the Gulf Stream, cyclones, tornadoes, and hurricanes, and also affects the course of flying objects. If you launch a rocket from the North Pole directly at San Francisco without accounting for the drift of the Coriolis Effect, it will land somewhere in the Pacific Ocean.

You don't have to be a specialist to benefit from the metaffective uses of the principle. Did you ever try to progress toward a goal while everything pertinent to your activity seemed to be changing speeds on you? This can be as disconcerting as walking on a spinning disk. You might feel disoriented, as if the ground beneath your feet were tugging you in unanticipated directions. You lose your psychological bearings and are prone to flying off course, because it's hard to adapt to the changes. Now, when such conditions arise, you have a name for them: "I'm really discombobulated. I've been totally knocked off balance by the Coriolis Effect."

This metaffect can also be used in problem-solving situations. You can visualize the process of solving a problem as being equivalent to traveling across the surface of a spinning object, like earth or a carousel, different parts of which move at different rates of speed. Recalling the Coriolis Effect, you can be prepared when circumstances force you to make decisions that are analogous to veering in one direction or another. At times, the very foundation on which you've built your solution may seem to shift. Now you can say, "We're being coriolised left and right. Let's stop and rethink this. We have to adjust quickly or we'll be so far off course we'll never reach our goal."

Perhaps the most helpful metaffective use is to account for the fact that our best-laid plans often fail because we have not taken the Coriolis Effect into account. We save three years for a trip to Paris, but by the time we arrive the prices have moved beyond what we initially budgeted. Or while we are getting a new product ready for the market, the world keeps turning, and by the time our goods arrive on the shelves, the potential buyers are ready to throw them in the ocean. In fact, Detroit automakers are constantly coriolised by their Japanese counterparts. Because the Japanese are able to develop new cars twice as fast as Americans, their standards are like moving targets—Detroit designers take aim, and by the time their products reach their mark, the Japanese are once again three years ahead.

As nothing in this spinning world holds its place, when making plans we need to know as best we can where things will be in the future, not where they are today.

The Coriolis Effect can also serve as a useful reminder of the importance of inner tranquility. Spinning disks and spheres evoke a whirligig image of life in constant motion, faster and wilder at the periphery, where we address our material desires, and slower and quieter in toward the center of one's being, what T. S. Eliot called "the still point of the turning world." Our innermost core—the equivalent of the center of a carousel or the axis of a whirling sphere—is where we can find the serenity and sure footing of pure silence. That is the still point to which one can retreat when the Coriolis Effect starts pulling one's life off course.

Coulomb's Law

Two bodies, powerfully charged, are drawn to each other by some mysterious primal force. As they move closer together, the strength of the attraction grows exponentially. Each time the distance between them is reduced by half, the attraction multiplies by a factor of four, and soon the electric charge pulses through the bodies like the power that drives the sun.

Leave it to a Frenchman to discover such an erotic-sounding principle. No, not Rimbaud or Charles Aznavour, but Charles Augustin de Coulomb, the eighteenth-century physicist for whom the unit of quantity of an electric charge, the coulomb, is named. And Coulomb was talking not about sexual energy, but about electrons.

Coulomb's Law, which was discovered in 1785, helps describe the forces that bind electrons to a nucleus, that lock the atoms in molecules, and that hold together solids and liquids. The law states that the electrostatic force between two charged bodies is proportional to the product of the amounts of electrical charge on the bodies divided by the square of the distance between them. For example, if you halve the distance between the bodies, the strength of the electric force quadruples. If the bodies are of opposite charges, one negative and one positive, they will be attracted to each other (*vive la différence*), whereas if they are similarly charged, the force between them is repulsive.

Coulomb, being French, would probably be pleased if we appropriated his law and applied it metaffectively to romance. Following the homily "out of sight, out of mind," if you double your distance from a loved one, the strength of the electric field between you diminishes by a factor of four; that is, it will be reduced to one-quarter of its earlier force. A love affair that ends because a long separation cooled the flame beyond rekindling might thus be said to have succumbed to Coulomb's Law: "We tried to keep it alive, but it wasn't meant to be. Each week we were apart, the attraction became twice as weak. I'm afraid Coulomb's Law was just too strong for us."

The effect also occurs when two people are so much alike that they actually repel each other like electrons of similar charges: "I can't stand being around him. He's so much like me, it spooks me into this coulomb reaction and I have to run away." On the other hand, the metaffect also evokes a highly charged affair in which the force of attraction gets stronger as one body inches toward the other and reaches the power of infinity when the advancing parties connect: "When I'm near you, darling, I can't help myself. I get all charged up by Coulomb's Law." And then later, deep in the night, perhaps this corollary would apply: "It's been absolutely incredible, but I'm coulombed out. Let's spend some time apart and recharge our electrons."

If you take "opposite charges" to mean contrary character traits, then the metaphor rings even truer, since the clash of opposites often ignites wilder, more elemental passion than the gentle compatibility of similar personalities: "My boyfriend and I have nothing in common, but as soon as we're in the same room together Coulomb's Law takes over and the sparks fly."

This metaffect can also come in handy for singles. The next time you're at a party or bar and you see a stranger across a crowded room, and that familiar electric tingle courses through your nervous system, and you walk slowly toward that alluring creature, and you feel the power of attraction doubling with each step until your eyes meet and you're inches away and it's make-it-or-break-it time and you have to say something you hope won't sound dumb or corny or overly lascivious, you now have the perfect line: "Hello. Do you believe in Coulomb's Law?"

The Crown Prince Syndrome

In her book *The Yin & Yang of Organizations,* management expert Nancy Foy describes how certain firms develop managerial talent: "A number of companies have 'A lists' of young managers who have been identified as having particularly high potential. These people usually get enriched opportunities to try their wings. They are moved around faster, counseled more often, sent on more courses, and have the best possible chances to acquire mentors, organizational know-how, and a sense of opportunity."

Foy cautions executives that this approach can be trouble-

some because of what she terms the *Crown Prince Syndrome.* The problem, she says, is that in most organizations people have ways of finding out who is on the A-list and who is not. Those who are on it tend to gain an extra measure of confidence from the special treatment they receive, whereas those left off the list frequently become demoralized, perhaps even embittered. As a result, their motivation diminishes, they lose their dedication, and their potential ends up being wasted.

Adding the Crown Prince Syndrome to your vocabulary will help you recognize the condition if it manifests in your organization. When Fred or Fanny Fastrack is shifted to a position favorable for advancement, or gets sent to a training seminar in Acapulco, or receives frequent invitations to lunch with Mr. Mentor, now you know what to tell your confidants: "I may have to put in for a transfer. It looks like the Crown Prince Syndrome is reigning in my department."

If you're on the rise, you may want to know early in the game whether the syndrome is operating in your organization and, if it is, what you can do to be crowned. And, when considering a new job, you might candidly ask a colleague, "Does this company promote by the Crown Prince Syndrome? If so, who does the crowning and how do you get to be a prince?" (Actually, it may not be too difficult to find out how to make the A-list. Most companies evidently tend to promote a certain type—those most like the people at the top. Consciously or not, subordinates have a tendency to mimic the mannerisms, gestures, style of dress, and other characteristics of those in power, and the ones who do it well are most likely to be singled out for advancement.)

If you're a manager, you might want to caution department supervisors about crowning too many princes and making known the identities of those in such an aristocracy. "I want you all to guard against the Crown Prince Syndrome. It's bad for morale, and we might end up turning off some talented people."

As a metaffect, the concept can be extended beyond its organizational origins to other contexts in which a particular person or group is singled out for special treatment. For example, watch out for doctors and nurses who spend more time with certain patients, or teachers who give extra attention to their "pets." Parents might want to call the syndrome to the attention of the principal: "I'm afraid Ms. McQueen is spending so much time grooming her gifted crown princes for the Ivy League that my daughter and her classmates are being ignored."

Politicians too can use the metaffect as a graphic synonym for questionable practices such as nepotism and favoritism. I can hear the campaign speeches now: "If I am elected, I promise there will be no Crown Prince Syndrome during my administration."

The Doppler Effect

The next time you are in a train station, listen for the *Doppler Effect*. As a train approaches, the sound you hear will have a higher and higher pitch; when the train passes and speeds away, the pitch will become lower. The change in pitch is caused by the alteration in the frequency of the sound waves as the distance between the source (the moving train) and you (the receiver) changes.

The effect is named for Christian Doppler, an Austrian scientist who discovered it in 1842. Since then, it has been demonstrated with light waves as well as sound and has been put to use in radar (the police know your car is speeding because of it), in astronomy, and for a host of other practical purposes.

Here's how the Doppler Effect occurs with light. The frequency of light waves correspond to what we perceive as a color; the lowest frequencies are on the red end of the spectrum (infrared) and the highest are on the blue end (ultraviolet). So, an object emits a wave of light that reaches our eyes as a certain color. As the object moves toward us, the light waves emitted reach us faster than they did when it was farther away, which means that the number of waves we receive per second (the frequency) will be higher. The light will therefore appear to be bluer as the object approaches. If the object moves away from us, the frequency we receive will be lower and the light will appear more red.

The Doppler Effect was instrumental in the advancement of astronomy. By recognizing the "blue shift" and "red shift" of heavenly bodies, astronomers were able to calculate the velocity and rotation of stars and galaxies.

Having the Doppler Effect in your vocabulary will not only help you impress your companions on train platforms and starry nights; it can also be of service in a variety of settings where perception and distance are involved. For instance, when something or someone moves away from us—physically or mentally—our recalled perception of the "color" or "tone" of that object or person changes. (Absence makes the heart grow fonder as surely as distance makes the light grow redder and the pitch grow lower.) Metaffectively speaking, distance and time often seem to red-shift the mind, making events seem a bit rosier than they actually were.

When I think back to a childhood spent in the streets of Brooklyn, I am dopplered into fond recollection of boisterous family gatherings, endless hours of stickball, Dodger games at Ebbets Field, hot dogs and thrills at Coney Island, the smell of fingerpaint in a classroom, and my first crush on a girl. Somehow, the incessant urban noise, the dirt, the dearth of open spaces and anything green, the cockroaches, the black eyes and bloody noses, getting mugged, and even having my first crush obnoxiously rebuffed are all red-shifted in my memory by the Doppler Effect of time.

When recalling long-gone romances or travels, we tend to remember the roses, not the thorns. We remember the scent of a lover's hair or the look in a lover's eyes, not the bickering and the aggravation and the pain. We gaze longingly at slides of cathedrals, cafés, and Doric columns and fondly recall the delightful people we met on the road, while the Doppler Effect filters out the lost luggage, larcenous cab drivers, jet lag, and indigestion: "I'm afraid the Doppler Effect has jarred your memory, dear. The truth is, we had a miserable time in Rome."

Consider the metaffect with respect to separation from a loved one who departs on a business trip. He moves farther and farther away, like a receding star. Your emotional palate becomes dopplerized; it gets redder, suggesting the heat of unexpressed passion, the anguish of longing, the anxious fear that perhaps he will never return. The soundtrack in your mind is similarly dopplered; the tones plummet to the range of cellos, suggesting despondence and melancholy: "I'm a total wreck. I was okay when Dave left, but I haven't heard from him in three days and the Doppler Effect has taken over."

Then there is the reverse scenario. Your beloved is coming home. As he draws nearer and nearer, the palate of your feelings gets bluer, suggesting the calmness that follows the release of tension, the contentment of knowing you are loved, the joy of blue-sky days ahead. The score is jubilant; it rises to the tone of a happy flute: "Dave is coming home. Every second, my perceptions are being dopplered into a state of joyous anticipation."

The Double Effect

Suppose you are driving a car, when suddenly a woman and two children dart into the street against the light. You slam on your brakes, but it's too late to stop in time. In a split-second thought, you realize you can yank the steering wheel to swerve out of the way, but in doing so you will run right into an old man standing on the curb. You do it. You hit the man in order to avoid killing a mother and two children.

The unfortunate result was foreseeable; you knew what would happen if you turned the wheel. The question is, should you be held responsible for the man's death? According to the *Double Effect*, no, you should not be considered blameworthy, because you did not *aim* to produce the effect. Your motive was not to hit the old man but to avoid hitting three others. The important factor is your positive intention as opposed to the disastrous side effect of your action.

The Double Effect is a principle of *casuistry,* a school of thought that seeks to apply general moral principles to particular cases. Associated with Christian theology as well as law and psychology, casuistry historically holds that morality cannot be viewed in absolute terms because every individual and every situation is unique. When rigid laws are applied too inflexibly to individual cases, hardship frequently results. One of the traditional casuist aims was to mitigate such overly rigid laws. However, because of the extreme positions taken by some of its adherents, casuistry has lost credence in modern times; in legal circles the term is used pejoratively for specious reasoning and an extreme tendency to excuse crimes.

As a metaffect, however, a principle that does not hold a person responsible for the side effects of well-intentioned actions is rich with potential. It might be used, for example, when you're tempted to make a harsh judgment about the actions of other people. We tend to see only the results of those actions— and not *all* the results at that—and too often we fail to ask ourselves *why* people do what they do. In some instances, they may have chosen the lesser of two evils. But, unaware of the larger evils that were averted, we judge people harshly.

For example, suppose you get stood up by a friend. You're sitting at the assigned meeting place, checking your watch and steaming, thinking that the person is an irresponsible, inconsiderate, self-centered jerk whom you will never have anything to do with again. What you may not be thinking is that maybe he had to disappoint you because he was giving CPR to an accident victim on the road or covering for a coworker who might otherwise have lost his job. "Consider this in the light of the Double Effect" might be a useful safeguard against premature judgments.

When your own actions stand to be judged unfairly, you

can use the metaffect as a defense: "I understand how you feel, Mr. Roberts, but if you analyze it according to the Double Effect, you can see that I'm not really to blame. If I had kept your secret, our clients would have withdrawn their business and everyone would have lost their jobs. I had to choose the lesser evil."

Although radical casuists might take the principle too far on occasion, the Double Effect is certainly a valid form of reasoning in certain everyday situations. As such, it could be worth teaching children: "I'm sure you deserved the prize, honey, but sometimes teachers have to do things that seem unfair in order to do something good for others. You've won so many prizes; the other kids should have a chance to feel good about themselves too." (You should watch out, though, for those times when your kids turn the Double Effect on you: "I wasn't wrong, Daddy. Remember when you had to hurt Kevin to stop him from beating up that little boy? That's sort of what I did.")

The Double Effect might help you achieve a certain equanimity in the face of life's seemingly inequitable annoyances and disappointments. For example:

Your new landlord takes over your apartment and forces you to move to more costly environs. Perhaps he's not just a greedy, money-grubbing scoundrel; maybe he had to do it to support his family or make the space available for a worthy cause.

You rush to purchase the used car of your dreams only to find that somone has beaten you to it. Instead of lamenting your hard luck, consider the possibility that the other guy might have needed the car more than you do.

You don't get the assignment you craved. Maybe the decision-maker wasn't out to screw you because she envies your success; perhaps the person who got it needed a break, just as you did when you were getting started.

In a larger sense, the Double Effect can provide a more

congenial perspective on the arcane mysteries of life. When, like Job in the Old Testament, you are stricken by a series of catastrophes that you can't possibly deserve and the universe seems to be one big kangaroo court stacked against you, by recalling this metaffect you can evoke a more positive assessment of the situation. Instead of "Why are these horrible things happening to me?" you might think, "Maybe if this hadn't happened to me, something far worse would have happened to many more people, perhaps even to those I love. Maybe the universe functions according to some Double Effect system of justice."

We may never know for certain whether the universe operates by a cosmic Double Effect. Nevertheless, it might be more comforting to believe that it does, rather than to assume that the gods—or the laws of nature or whatever runs the show—are capricious, arbitrary, and sometimes malicious.

The Eureka Effect

Archimedes was a Greek mathematician, inventor, and physicist whose road to posterity began with a simple request and ended in a bathtub. Hiero II, king of Syracuse, asked Archimedes to determine whether the royal crown was made of pure gold or alloyed with silver. Unable to come up with a way to solve the problem, the frustrated scientist retired to his home to relax in a bath. When he submerged, the water in the tub overflowed and, according to this tale, he suddenly realized that the amount of water being displaced was equal to the volume of his immersed body. His mind instantly connected this insight to the conundrum of the king's crown.

Because gold is very dense, a pure piece of the metal that weighs two pounds takes up less space than a two-pound chunk of silver. Therefore, if you were to submerge two pounds of gold, it would displace less water than two pounds of silver, because the gold occupies less volume. Now Archimedes had a way to determine whether the king's crown had been adulterated. He could weigh the crown and match it with an equal weight of pure gold, then submerge the crown and the gold weight in separate tubs. If the crown was pure gold, it would displace the exact same amount of water as the weight. But if it displaced *more* water than the gold, it would clearly be an alloy (which, in fact, it turned out to be).

So electrified was Archimedes by this flash of insight that he leaped from the tub and ran naked through the streets of Syracuse, shouting, "Eureka!"—which means "I have found it." Over the centuries, the word has come to signify any sudden discovery, particularly one of a triumphant nature—from the flash of gold in a panhandler's pan to the flash of intuition that answers a nettlesome question.

The *Eureka Effect* has been identified as a common feature of scientific discovery, artistic creation, problem-solving, and decision-making. Typically, breakthroughs in those arenas follow the same pattern as Archimedes' triumph. The search for an answer to a puzzle often begins with analysis of the problem and consideration of tried-and-true methods. If those fail, the frustrated problem-solver inevitably has to get away from the conundrum, if only to sleep or eat (or, as Archimedes did, to bathe). And then, often when least expected, the answer suddenly pops into awareness, the pieces of the puzzle having presumably been pulled together by a diligent subconscious.

The next time you make a sudden, brilliant discovery, you

can shed light on the moment by declaring (while fully dressed, one hopes), "Ladies and gentlemen, you have just witnessed the Eureka Effect in action."

The metaffect has practical implications. Researchers note that illuminative insight is usually preceded by a period of "incubation," during which time the mind is not consciously engaged in the problem at hand. We disregard incubation at our peril when our zeal for answers drives us to continue working way past the point where fatigue renders our efforts futile. And so, next time you are faced with a difficult conundrum, remember Archimedes and the long line of artists, inventors, and scientists who followed in his dripping footsteps. Take a walk in the woods, or a nap, or jog around the block, or, indeed, sink into a nice hot bath. If colleagues or bosses look askance, wondering why your nose is not pressed to the grindstone, accusing you of goldbricking and trying to make you feel guilty, you can retort, "There's a scientific explanation for this, Mr. Smith. It's the best way to stimulate the Eureka Effect."

And imagine how popular you'll be among your colleagues when you stand up at a tense conference and say, "This situation calls for the Eureka Effect. Let's get the hell out of this stuffy office and go to the ball game."

Fabian Tactics

Have you ever faced an imminent battle with your boss, or a friend, or your spouse, or your parents, only to get the strong feeling that maybe you ought not enter the fray at all? Rather than feel like a coward at such moments, you can look at it this way: maybe something is telling you that, in this case at least, fighting fire with fire is not the best strategy for gaining victory. There is a historic precedent for this: *Fabian Tactics.*

The term is named for Quintus Fabius Maximus, a Roman general who achieved lasting fame by fending off the mighty Carthaginian army during the Second Punic War. Led by Hannibal, one of the great military leaders in history, the Carthaginians had crossed the Alps into the Italian peninsula in 218 B.C. and proceeded to conquer one city after another, vanquishing Roman forces vastly superior in number. But when General Fabius took over command of Roman military operations, he tried a new set of tactics. Convinced that doing battle with Hannibal was a futile venture, Fabius would station forces near the Carthaginians but refrain from engaging in customary warfare. Instead, whenever Hannibal's main army appeared, the Romans cut and ran. The general would then have his troops harass the enemy, cut off supply convoys, and attack stragglers. The tactics earned Fabius the moniker *Cunctator,* Latin for "delayer."

Thanks to the Cunctator, the English language acquired the word *Fabian,* which the American Heritage Dictionary defines as "using or characterized by a cautious strategy of gradual social progress and avoidance of direct confrontation with the state." One notable use of the term came in 1884, when a group of British socialists, including George Bernard Shaw, adopted it for their new organization. Repudiating the revolutionary theory of Marxism, the Fabian Society opposed the notion that violent class struggle is necessary, opting instead for a program of gradual social reform.

Without necessarily knowing the historical precedent, many of us already use Fabian Tactics—delaying, harrassing, doing the unexpected, acting indirectly and unpredictably to achieve our objectives—in a number of competitive settings. Lawyers delay the start of a negotiation to give opponents the false impression that they are frightened or unprepared. Executives release surprise announcements to agitate or confuse their foes, thereby rendering their judgments less astute and their perceptions less accurate. Politicians use public innuendo to disarm adversaries and divert them from the real point of attack.

One small company used Fabian Tactics to lull a major competitor into a false sense of security. Knowing that a huge conglomerate was testing a product that would compete with its own, the company pulled its own merchandise from the shelves. The move had the appearance of being a declaration of defeat, but in fact more subtle, Fabianlike thinking was behind it. With less competition on the shelves, the conglomerate's test appeared to be a resounding success, giving them such inflated sales projections that they overspent, overproduced, and overpriced their product. Soon they were piling up red ink while the smaller company went on selling as before.

Fabian Tactics are especially useful in personal confrontations. Suppose you are confronted by an enraged adversary. Instead of meeting fire with fire, your best option might be to keep your cool in hopes of throwing him off balance. You might disarm him by doing something totally incongruous, such as asking an absurd question, offering a cup of tea, or cracking a joke. If your variations on Fabian Tactics do not diminish your opponent's hostility, they might at least confuse and frustrate him so much that you gain the upper hand.

Or, say you are just getting into a fight with your lover. Instead of trying to outshout him as usual, instead of defending yourself or trying to shift the blame, you can do a magic trick or a tap dance or tell a totally unrelated story. Later, in the afterglow of love, you can explain, "It wasn't ridiculous at all, it was a Fabian Tactic, and it worked, didn't it?"

At an earlier stage of romance, a crafty Fabian Tactic might be to play hard-to-get. If you think the object of your desire is the type to be turned off by an overeager pursuit, you might want to feign indifference in hope that doing so will make you appear more intriguing: "I'm not going to call. I know it's risky, but I think this case calls for Fabian Tactics."

Naturally, Fabian Tactics are not always appropriate. They worked on the Carthaginians for about ten years, but then the Roman citizens began to wonder if the general's strategy wasn't merely an excuse for timidity. Fearing that Rome was slowly bleeding to death as the war with Hannibal persisted, they eventually replaced Fabius with Scipio Aficanus, a young fire-brand who favored more aggressive tactics. Scipio also avoided Hannibal, but for a different reason: he launched an attack on Carthage itself, forcing Hannibal to give up the Italian cam-paign and defend his homeland. Ultimately, Scipio got the credit for defeating the invader. But would he have succeeded without the decade-long Fabian Tactics that preceded his cam-paign?

Bear in mind that using Fabian Tactics might entail a tempo-rary loss of face; your strategy could easily be interpreted as cowardice. Now you can set your detractors straight with a solid historic reference and an impressive new vocabulary item: "Me? Chicken? Ha! I'm simply using a time-honored strategy: Fabian Tactics."

If needed, you can add a macho reference: "Hey, like Mu-hammed Ali once said, 'Float like a butterfly, sting like a bee.'" Instead of slugging it out with the brutish Sonny Liston, Ali (then Cassius Clay) used Fabian Tactics of a sort, and the be-fuddled Liston wore himself out flailing away at a taunting moving target.

You can further support your argument by pointing out that the great Japanese warriors who created the code of the Samu-rai maintained that the true goal in any confrontation is to win without having to engage in actual battle. The ultimate Fabian

Tactic was well expressed by the Chinese philosopher, Sun-Tzu: "To win one hundred victories in one hundred battles is not the highest skill. To subdue the enemy without fighting is the highest skill."

The False Consensus Effect

Do you get annoyed by statements such as "But everybody feels that way" and "Everyone knows that"? They imply that if you don't feel what "everybody" feels, or if you happen *not* to know whatever it is that everyone supposedly knows, you are either a weirdo or hopelessly ill-informed. Most infuriating is when a conviction such as "Everyone feels that way" is based on nothing more than the careless assumption or wishful thinking of the person making the remark, who finds comfort in numbers.

Psychologists Gary Marks and Norman Miller have named phenomenon the *False Consensus Effect,* the tendency for people to believe that their own desires, beliefs, and even personal problems are shared by the majority.

Writing about the False Consensus Effect, psychologist Carol Tavris notes, "By overestimating the degree of agreement between themselves and others, people maintain their self-esteem, reduce the discomfort of inconsistency or feeling 'weird,' and maintain their self-righteousness." Tavris recalls the Iran-Contra hearings as an example of how the phenomenon can manifest in public affairs. When the media quoted poll results indicating that 70 percent of Americans considered Colonel Oliver North a hero, large numbers of dissenters accepted that and began to question their own convictions. However, it turned out that the polls were not scientific surveys; rather, the public had been invited to phone in their opinions, and the lines were flooded by North fans. In fact, says Tavris, other surveys showed that "70% of all Americans think Oliver North is a liar and a crook." Those who registered their affection for the colonel in all likelihood believed that their view reflected the prevailing national sentiment.

The False Consensus Effect is one reason that the price of democracy is eternal vigilance. A false consensus can curtail debate and the free flow of ideas by creating the impression that agreement has been achieved when in fact it has not. It can even trigger a self-fulfilling prophecy. An unpopular view might gather momentum because its adherents believe their support to be greater than it is, thus actually garnering that support when large numbers of people fall in step with the herd to avoid being different (see the Bandwagon Effect). Naturally, when people with minority opinions persuade themselves and others that they represent the majority, the illusion confers upon them a false sense of power, while those with contrary views are deflated by the belief that they are outnumbered. The "Moral Majority" became an instant force in American politics by its clever choice of name, which convinced followers and antagonists alike that their support was greater than it later turned out to be.

Now that you have a name for the phenomenon, you might be less likely to accept at face value someone's false consensus. Consider, for example, a coworker who claims that everyone in the department sides with his views on a proposed decision. You might challenge him with, "Have you taken an objective survey, or are you creating a False Consensus Effect?"

When your child tries to loosen your purse strings by telling you that "all the kids in school have a (name your commodity)," you might have her count the actual number that do, adding, "As your mother, I won't let you be suckered into a False Consensus Effect."

Of course, publicists use the False Consensus Effect by taking liberties with the term "best-seller" and with ads for movies that gather carefully selected phrases from reviewers to create the false impression of a positive critical consensus. The next time you see one of these, ask yourself whether the implied consensus is true or false. (If "best-seller" is written on the cover of this book, however, believe it.)

Perhaps the greatest vigilance needs to be directed at our own False Consensus Effects. It's easy to believe your own propaganda and to assume that everyone who matters (since they are all intelligent, compassionate, and wise) agrees with you. Reputations have been destroyed and businesses ruined by such assumptions. Perhaps the ubiquitous use of market surveys is a way to guard business decisions from the False Consensus Effect.

But polls won't help when the effect creates annoying family misunderstandings: "But, I thought we *all* wanted to go to the symphony," you bemoan incredulously. "These tickets cost two hundred bucks!"

"I'm afraid you created a False Consensus Effect, dear," says your spouse. "We want to see the Ice Capades."

The Fiddle Factor

Louis Dawson, an experienced mountain climber, told me about the *Fiddle Factor:* "In mountaineering, you encounter this with novices. It describes the endless, almost neurotic fooling around with gear while on the trail or a climb. Like taking your gloves off so you can change your sunglasses. Then one glove falls in the snow. Then another cloud bank comes in, so you take off your sunglasses. Then you decide to take a drink. Then you get cold from standing around, so you decide to take off your pack and put on more clothing. Then the effort of adjusting your pack makes you start to overheat, so you decide to remove that extra layer. Then the sun comes out, so you stop and put on some sunscreen because you forgot to put it on before you left camp. Then it's lunch time. . . ."

The Fiddle Factor occurs when novices are thrown into an alien, potentially hostile environment with a lot of unfamiliar paraphernalia (in the case of mountaineering, climbing gear, eating utensils, sun protection, etc.). As a result, they end up fiddling around with all the little things that experienced people take for granted. To the veterans in the group, the Fiddle Factor is maddening. It causes so many unnecessary delays that experts and guides practically want to jump off a cliff. And in avalanche conditions, or when a storm is moving toward the peak, Fiddle Factor delays can be quite hazardous.

As a metaffect, the term might be applied to any reasonably complex activity in which superfluous fiddling occurs. Studies of problem-solving in a variety of disciplines have shown that novices who are unfamiliar with tools, procedures, and protocol have to think about every little thing that goes into a task. This not only consumes time but diverts mental energy that could be devoted to creative thought.

Take, for example, a jazz musician picking up a new instrument or playing in a new band. With his attention absorbed by small things such as fingering and the habits of his fellow musicians, he is not as free to improvise. A secretary using a new word-processing program has to fiddle with simple commands

and differences in keyboard layout, thus cutting down typing speed. A traveler in a foreign land can't get as much done as a native, because she has to fiddle with strange currency, phrase books, and maps. A driver behind the wheel of a new car has to fiddle with the gear shift, the ventilation, the position of the seat, and other little items. But once the novice phase is over, the musician, the secretary, the traveler, the driver, or anyone else can perform the basic tasks automatically, without consciously having to attend to them. As a result, speed increases and the quality of performance generally improves. One might even say that evolving out of the Fiddle Factor is one of the things that makes an expert an expert.

Perhaps the Fiddle Factor is one reason why so many new businesses fail. An entrepreneur entering uncharted territory might underestimate the amount of time that goes into fiddling with unanticipated chores that weren't in the business plan. Meanwhile, the bills mount and the revenues don't match the projections. Now, would-be tycoons can reassure their families and creditors (at the risk of being compared to Nero): "Once we get past the Fiddle Factor, everything will move ahead as planned; I'm sure of it."

Now that you know about the Fiddle Factor, you might be able to avert the hassles it inevitably creates. If you're a beginner at something, you might try getting the rudiments down more quickly, and you might be more considerate of the veterans who have to twiddle their fingers while you fiddle. Conversely, when you become annoyed by a neophyte in your midst, knowing there's a name for the delays he or she causes will help you get through the inconvenience and perhaps speed things up: "Look, Samantha, I know you're new at this. Let me show you how to cut down on the Fiddle Factor so we can move ahead more rapidly."

When a new secretary arrives at the office, or a new worker checks in at the factory, or your spouse breaks in a new hobby, you can use this metaffect to soothe nerves jangled by interruptions, distractions, and mishaps: "Don't let it get to you; it's just the Fiddle Factor." Or, "We're all going to work overtime so we get past the Fiddle Factor phase by the first of the year."

If you're a parent who has ever tried to put together a kid's toy or a bicycle, you will want to lobby manufacturers to include a research-based Fiddle Factor on all labels and boxes. Something like:

Actual Assembly Time—2 hours
Fiddle Factor—4 hours
Total—6 hours

The Fosbury Flop

Not very long ago, high jumpers had a standard method of leaping over bars. They took a running start, kicked off with their lead leg, and straddled the bar sideways, face down. With this technique, high jumping evolved to where the world record was in the neighborhood of seven-and-a-half feet. But progress was idling at around that height.

Then, along come Dick Fosbury. In the late 1950s and early 1960s he was an obscure Oregon schoolboy, a gawky kid whose coach tried to get him to take up another sport or dump the absurd jumping style he'd made up on his own. For Dick Fosbury did not jump like anyone else. You might say he literally bent over backward to be different: rather than straddle the bar, Fosbury planted his leg, twisted his body, and thrust into the air backward, with his arm and shoulder leading the way. He cleared the bar head first and "flopped" over it with his face up and his arched back turned toward the ground. This highly unorthodox, weird-looking style came to be known as the *Fosbury Flop*.

As it turns out, the flop was no flop. Nor was it a mere

curiosity and Dick Fosbury a Cepheid Variable (see page 50). He took his act to Mexico City for the 1968 Olympic Games and won the gold medal, setting an Olympic record in the process.

In short order, this new twist in high-jumping technique caught on. It turned out to be easier to perform, required less training to master, and allowed for higher jumping. By the time the 1972 Olympics rolled around, the Fosbury Flop was the method of choice around the world. Dwight Stones, the next American to shine in the high jump, flopped over head first and backward, as did his competitors and successors. Today, the straddle-style jump is as rare at a track meet as a cello at a rock concert, and the world record is just over eight feet, an unthinkable height in the days of the straddle jump.

The Fosbury Flop was a conceptual breakthrough by someone with the audacity to question assumptions that everyone else took for granted, the vision to think of an alternative, and the courage to persist with his unorthodoxy in the face of ridicule. As such, it can be used as a metaffect for other innovations, particularly ones that shatter barriers and become the new norms.

Sports are filled with Fosbury Flops. In basketball, the flat-footed, two-handed set shot, which now seems laughably quaint, was the standard for sharpshooters back in the forties. Then a Stanford player named Hank Lusetti invented the jump shot. In football, extra points and field goals were always kicked with the toe of the shoe, not the instep, and place-kickers approached the ball straight-on rather than from the side—until a European soccer player named Pete Gogolak tried it a different way. Shotputters used to stand still, take a quarter-turn of their bodies, and heave the shot. Then Perry O'Brian stood in the back of the circle and took two steps forward before cutting loose. O'Brian's method, called "the glide," won him a gold medal in the 1952 Olympics. By 1956 it was the standard.

At the risk of sounding irreverent, you might say that the history of science is marked by Fosbury Flops: Copernicus postulating that the sun, not the earth, was the center of the solar system; Newton linking a falling apple to the motion of heavenly bodies; Einstein asking why we assume that time and space are absolutes; Watson and Crick configuring DNA as a double helix.

The history of the arts is a history of Fosbury Flops: Picasso fosburied artistic conventions repeatedly throughout his lengthy career, flopping the forms of everyday perception on their sides, backs, and heads; Charlie Parker fosburied American music when he loosened the constraints on jazz; photography took a Fosbury Flop into motion pictures when Eadweard Muybridge lined up a bank of cameras and captured sequential shots of a galloping horse; Agnes de Mille did a Fosbury Flop on the musical theater when she interjected ballet form to the choreography of *Oklahoma* in 1943.

The metaffect might help you to inspire innovative thinking. Are you stuck for a solution to a nagging problem, or mired in inertia while the clock ticks on an important opportunity? Does your gut tell you there must be a better way, even while your mind wraps itself around the tried and true? Remember the Flop: "Okay, gang, let's fosbury this problem. Turn it on its head, give it a radical twist, and take a leap forward."

Here are some other metaffective applications for various professions.

(*For hairdressers*) "You need a whole new image. What if I gave you a Fosbury Flop?"

(*For politicians*) "What the Middle East needs is another Anwar Sadat to come along and fosbury this stalemate."

(*For editors and producers*) "The story is one predictable cliché after another. Tell the writer the plot needs a Fosbury Flop."

(*For travel agents*) "Why not do something different this year? Let me work out a Fosbury Flop for your vacation."

Whenever radical departures, innovative techniques, or conceptual breakthroughs are needed, the spirit and letter of the Fosbury Flop can vault you over the top.

Fourier's Theorem

After fighting for Napoleon in North Africa, Jean Baptiste Joseph Fourier was named governor of a portion of Egypt, but it was mainly for his scientific achievements that he was made a baron. A mathematician renowned for his research on numerical equations, Fourier made major contributions to our understanding of vibratory motion and sound waves. One concept known as *Fourier's Theorem,* which he discovered in 1807, states that any wave, no matter how complex or unusual, can be reproduced by combining a number of sine waves of different amplitudes, frequencies, and phases.

A sine wave, the simplest, most elementary type of wave, is repetitive and periodic. Sine waves look like this:

Fourier's principle applies to waves of water, waves of light, waves of sound, and all other wave phenomena. Music, for example, is composed of complex sound waves in the air. Theoretically, you can reproduce any song by combining a certain number of pure sine waves of a particular amplitude and frequency. This is analogous to saying that any collection of words, from a simple sentence like "See Dick run" to the collected works of Shakespeare, is made up of a certain combination of twenty-six letters.

Thanks to Fourier's insight, scientists are able to break down complex shapes and patterns and display them in simple charts called Fourier Transforms. Variations of the procedure are used in photography, sound technology, satellite transmission, medicine, and a host of other endeavors.

Fourier's Theorem essentially enables one to break down a complex phenomenon into its simpler constituent parts. Metaffectively, this is a fertile concept. Imagine telling your attorney or your insurance agent, "Can you do a Fourier Transform on this contract, please? This is way too complicated for me." Most Americans would not object to having some of their tax dollars used to create a Fourier Department in Washington, D.C., which would translate long-winded political speeches and incomprehensible government documents into simple, understandable synopses.

Now, armed with this metaffect, you can say when someone rambles on interminably with a convoluted tale, "Can you fourier this story, please? I don't have all day."

Executives might find the term useful in business, as in "From now on this department will be run on Fourier principles. All complicated items will be reproduced as succinct statements that everyone can understand" or "Listen, Steve, I don't have time to read this whole report. Can you do a Fourier Analysis and give me the essence in some charts and graphs?"

Transforming the long and complex into the short and simple is done all the time, of course. Politicians commonly have their staffs boil down lengthy reports into brief summaries. Presumably, that is how the terms *briefing* and *debriefing* originated.

In Hollywood, too, busy executives seldom read scripts; they have readers prepare a brief synopsis and character breakdown for quick consumption. Now, if you're a movie mogul and an agent swears that the script in his hot little hands is the greatest thing since *Casablanca,* you can call in your lovely assistant and, instead of issuing a mundane, commonplace directive like "Get me coverage on this script," you can demonstrate your erudition by saying something that the agent won't soon forget: "Sweetheart, can you do a quick Fourier Transform on this?"

Actually, you might fourier that "coverage" even further, breaking the story down to the pithiest possible statement, the sort of one-liner used in *TV Guide* listings. Since, in Hollywood, brevity is the soul of business if not wit, producers and writers are advised to come up with such "log lines" when pitching their wares to executives who have no time to listen to entire stories, much less read scripts. Good log lines titillate the potential buyer by suggesting how the eventual show might be advertised. When asked, for example, how he would pitch *The Graduate* to someone who hadn't seen the film, one Fourier expert replied, "How do you tell the girl you're in love with that you've been sleeping with her mother?"

The Gambler's Fallacy

Nine times in a row, the coin toss has come up heads. Now the same coin is tossed in the air for the tenth time. What is your call?

Most people would call tails, on the grounds that the law of averages is bound to start evening out the score. Since the chances of a coin coming down heads are precisely equal to its chances of coming down tails, over time there ought to be an equal number of each. Therefore, most people conclude, the odds favor tails because it's about time to start balancing the score.

Alas, that reasoning is so erroneous it has been given a name: the *Gambler's Fallacy*. It is a mistake to assume that, on any given toss, either heads or tails is more likely to come up than the other. Even if the coin has come up heads ninety-nine times in a row, the odds are still fifty–fifty for the next toss. Mathematician Morris Kline says that the fallacy is persuasive because people think that the greater the deviation from a mean (i.e., the fifty–fifty ratio we expect from coins), the greater the restoring force will be *toward* the mean. But coins don't know from means and averages and odds. They are still half as likely to turn up tails. In fact, if a given coin blatantly defies probability by coming up heads over and over again, you would do well to bet that it will do so one more time, because it is probably a two-headed coin.

Although we should know better, we frequently make mistakes in judgment due to faulty notions of what is typical or representative. Watch amateur roulette players: if black has come up several times in a row, they will pile their chips on red. Unfortunately for them, such events are statistically independent; that is, each toss of a coin or spin of the wheel is statistically independent of what has happened before. Statistical events do not have memories; they are governed by the laws of probability.

In another, more tragic example of the misuse of probability, many soldiers during World War I took shelter in bomb craters, thinking that the odds were weighted heavily against another bomb hitting the same spot. That kind of reasoning was fatal in at least one case in the next war. After his London flat had been strafed by Nazi bombs, an Englishman named P. S. Milner-Barry returned to the dwelling, refusing to relocate. He insisted that the law of averages was in his favor, right up until his flat got bombed again—with him in it. Milner-Barry should have known more about probability: he was a chess master.

So, if your spouse uses your life savings to bet on red because it hasn't come up in a while, rather than merely threatening divorce or murder, you can shock him into submission by saying, "You're committing the Gambler's Fallacy!" A brief explanation will distract him long enough for you to pocket some chips. And, if you're lucky, the spin will come up black and your point will be proven.

Metaffectively, the principle is worth expanding into other arenas, where, for example, we rationalize our wishful thinking with dubious reference to the law of averages. If your spouse recently received a speeding ticket, don't let him flaunt the posted speed limit because he believes that his number can't come up again so quickly. There is no cosmic quota system for traffic tickets, and the judge won't accept the Gambler's Fallacy as a defense.

If your house has been shaken by an earthquake, pay no mind to your neighbor if he says there's no sense preparing for another tremblor because earthquakes, like lightning, do not strike the same place twice. Instead, tell him, "You can make the Gambler's Fallacy if you want, but I'm stocking up on water and canned food."

If you have four daughters, it is inadvisable to get pregnant again just because you really want a boy and you assume the odds are now in your favor. Ask your doctor whether the Gambler's Fallacy applies to genetics. And remember Jerry Lewis: Back in the fifties, after his wife had borne four sons, she got pregnant again, and Jerry started a "Think Pink" campaign among his fans. Alas, nature cared as little about Jerry's entreaties as it does about our erroneous calculations in roulette.

If you're attracted to someone who has been divorced four times, don't assume your union is destined to work out because only fifty percent of marriages end in divorce and the law of averages says it's time for the guy's score to balance out. See a counselor instead. A good one will tell you, "Don't succumb to the Gambler's Fallacy. This man has problems."

Gödel's Incompleteness Theorem

In geometry, you were given certain incontestable axioms, such as "Through any two points only one straight line can be drawn," and from that starting point you logically deduced any number of useful conclusions. The system is so neat and precise that scientists always dreamed that *all* arithmetical truths—maybe even all the laws of nature—could, in the same manner, be derived logically from a small set of basic assumptions.

In 1931, Kurt Gödel, a mathematician who was born in Czechoslovakia and worked in Vienna, blew the fantasy out of the water. Furthermore, as if to rub it in, he used flawless logic to expose the limits of logic itself. Gödel proved that knowledge derived from mathematical logic is inherently incomplete.

The way Gödel arrived at his theorem was ingenious. He turned systematic logic onto itself by using a mathematical hypothesis that stated, essentially, "Using logic, this hypothesis cannot be proved true." This was the equivalent of saying, "This statement is false." It leads to an inescapable contradiction.

Gödel's work showed that logical contradictions are inevitable if the mathematical system being employed is consistent. And since *inconsistent* logical systems are useless, every useful system is by its nature incomplete. That is the essence of *Gödel's Incompleteness Theorem,* a landmark in the history of knowledge—like the works of Copernicus, Newton, and Einstein—that overthrew cherished assumptions and forced the scientific enterprise to rethink itself.

The repercussions of Gödel's work have been enormous. It led some to a kind of existential resignation, because, if nothing can be known completely, the goal of fully comprehending the cosmos through reason alone is a pipe dream. If you want complete knowledge, the theorem implies, you have to look beyond formal systems of thought.

To others, Gödel's proof engendered a strange, new form of hope. In their eyes, the theorem legitimized subjectivity in the quest for knowledge, elevating truth-seeking to the realm of metaphysics and conferring a new credibility on previously disparaged modes of knowing—faith and direct, intuitive cognition.

For laypersons, Gödel's Theorem has interesting metaffective possibilities with respect to the uncertainties of life and the limits of our customary ways of knowing things. For example, since education is a formal system of sorts, a restless college student might declare to his parents, "I'm taking a year off to travel and experience life firsthand. According to Gödel's Incompleteness Theorem, no matter how hard I study, I'll never know anything completely through books and lectures."

The theorem has something similar to offer spiritual seekers. Oriental sages were onto something Gödel-like when they made their disciples read learned texts only to inform them afterward that reading learned texts is a useless endeavor, because ultimately, truth can be found only in the sacred chambers of the soul. As the Incompleteness Theorem suggests, you have to transcend the system itself if you want complete knowledge. This is probably why the Greeks (who also gave us geometry) exhorted seekers of truth to "First know thyself."

On a more earthly level, knowing about the Incompleteness Theorem can save you a lot of trouble when it comes to relationships. The desire to know another person completely and totally is powerful, but if you think you can really accomplish this, you might as well join Sisyphus rolling that rock uphill. Inevitably, the harder one tries to know another person perfectly, the more impossible the task becomes as mysteries compound enigmas, which multiply the conundrums. Remember Gödel and spare yourself the aggravation.

Metaffectively, the theorem also offers an erudite way to express skepticism. When someone you know gets wildly fanatical over some philosophy or belief system because he thinks it explains everything that ever perplexed him, sit him down and say, "I think you're getting a tad overzealous. Gödel's Incompleteness Theorem implies that no formal system can have all the answers."

And think of the fun you can have when confronted by someone with an overly developed left-brain hemisphere who prides himself on his fastidious (and in your mind obnoxious) use of logic, or when some pompous nerd at a party asserts that the only hope for knowing the whole truth about something is to reason it through as rigorously as would a computer. You can say, "I beg your pardon, but according to Gödel's Theorem, your formal logic is destined to be as incomplete as the voyage of the Titanic." Then, once you have him partly convinced, if you feel really mischievous, you can top off the repartee by stating, "Of course, my hypothesis can't be proved true," and stroll off to sample the hors d'oeuvres.

You might want to extend the notion of incompleteness beyond the things we know to the things we do. Everyone from artists in funky lofts to executives in sumptuous suites can relate to the old housewife's lament that the work is never done: "I'm a slave to Gödel's Theorem. Nothing ever seems complete."

And, on those occasions when you're sure you've thought of every possible thing that can go wrong, only to have the one thing you *didn't* think of ruin an entire enterprise, you can tell your colleagues, "Well, we should have known we hadn't thought of everything. There's just no escaping Gödel's Incompleteness Theorem."

The Greenhouse Effect

You've undoubtedly heard the term *Greenhouse Effect* by now. In simpler times, it might have conjured up images of white-coated horticulturists in glass-enclosed houses delicately tending plants that need controlled temperature and humidity. Those glass enclosures were called greenhouses because of all the greenery that sprouted and grew within their walls. Now the term strikes a more ominous chord: some of the gases our industrial civilization coughs and belches into the air have been trapping heat in the earth's atmosphere, causing our planet to heat up. If we're not careful, the coastlines will wash away and on land the operative color will be not green, but brown, as in parched fields and arid valleys.

According to some estimates, global mean temperatures may rise as many as 8 degrees by the year 2040. Within fifty years, the annual number of days on which the temperature surpasses 90 degrees in Washington, D.C., could go from 35 to 85, in Chicago from 16 to 56, and in Dallas from 100 to 162. If the heat rises in this manner, as scientists predict, the polar ice caps will melt and the oceans will swell, inundating large portions of terra firma.

To understand the effect, it is useful to know how a greenhouse works. When sunlight passes through its glass, all the objects inside the room warm up, just as they would if they were outside. However, warm objects send back some of their heat in the form of infrared radiation, most of which does not penetrate back through the walls, since glass is only slightly transparent to this wavelength. The heat instead gets reflected back inside. Everything within the glass enclosure thus gets hotter, which is why plants flourish even when it's cold outside.

Years ago, scientists drew an analogy to the earth. Our atmosphere consists mainly of oxygen, nitrogen, and argon, all of which are quite transparent to both visible light and infrared radiation. However, the atmosphere also contains 0.03 percent carbon dioxide, which, like greenhouse glass, is *not* very transparent to infrared. As a result, there is—and always has been—a Greenhouse Effect on earth. This was good until recently: it meant warm summer breezes and diaphanous dresses and night games and lemonade, because the earth was 15 to 20 degrees warmer than it would have been without that small amount of carbon dioxide to trap some of the heat.

For thousands of years, the earth did quite nicely under greenhouse conditions; the carbon-dioxide level in the atmosphere was never more than 28 parts per million. Then we started burning fossil fuels like profligate heirs burn money, spewing enormous amounts of carbon dioxide and other heat-trapping waste products into the air. We also destroyed rain forests that would have absorbed much of the carbon dioxide, and we invented chemical fertilizers, the internal combustion engine, refrigerators, and spray cans, all of which give off fumes that add to the atmospheric greenhouse. By 1958, the carbon-dioxide level was up to 315 parts per million; thirty years later it was 340. As a result, the earth is heating up—not as much as Venus, where there is so much carbon dioxide that the planet's surface temperature is way above the boiling point of water, but enough so that the future of the planet as a livable environment for humans is in question.

With this information in hand, you can now speak with some authority when someone at a party thinks the Greenhouse Effect is a way of explaining the presence of sun-dried tomatoes in the pasta. Moreover, the term has terrific metaffective possibilities.

Heat has long been a metaphor for emotional conditions, as in "The heat is on" and "Things are really heating up." Rather than such mundane expressions, you now have a more intriguing phrase for times when emotions rise. Say you're at a meeting and someone announces, "I just got word from headquarters. If we lose this account, we're sunk." As the sweat breaks out, you can inspire those around you by saying, "All right, the Greenhouse Effect has just kicked in. Try to keep your heads cool before your thinking caps melt."

Some other possibilities:

(For sportscasters) "They've tied the score. The stadium is in the grip of a massive Greenhouse Effect."

(For beleaguered spouses) "If you don't learn to leave your work at the office, you'll greenhouse the entire family."

(For the takeover artist) "Wait until I announce that we now own 51 percent of them. Their whole building will turn into one big greenhouse."

(For the single guy) "I stopped dating her. She's like a walking Greenhouse Effect. As soon as she enters a room, the guys heat up and the pollen count goes off the charts."

Of course, the term is about more than heat; it has to do with the introduction of noxious elements that change the environment from relatively healthy to dangerous. For example, suppose you're having a dispute with another party. Through a series of difficult but civilized negotiations, you reach the brink of a settlement. Then the other side calls in a lawyer and you are forced to do the same. Before you know it, the whole thing turns noxious, you end up in an ugly court battle, and your legal bills rise like the temperature in a greenhouse.

Applying the idea metaffectively to interpersonal relations, we can think of toxic emotions such as anger, hostility, resentment, and jealousy as the equivalent of smokestacks, chemical plants, and other polluters. Nasty remarks, dirty looks, and malicious gossip are the equivalent of carbon dioxide and chlorofluorocarbons (the stuff released by refrigerator coolants and spray cans). When these noxious elements build up in the atmosphere of a closed environment such as an office or home, the ambiance gets foul and heat builds up. Your cool composure starts to melt like the polar ice caps, flooding your system with adrenaline. The borders of your patience recede like the coastlines of the continents of earth.

At this point, you need to do for your social environment what all of us must do for our planet: stand up and shout, "Let's put a stop to this or the Greenhouse Effect will destroy us all!" Then you can introduce compassion, calmness, tolerance, and other nonpolluting energy sources.

Gresham's Law

Sir Thomas Gresham was a sixteenth-century English merchant and financier who served as economic advisor to Edward VI and Elizabeth I. A very wealthy man, Gresham was a principal figure in the founding of the Royal Exchange and is best remembered for the law that bears his name. In its familiar, pithy formulation, *Gresham's Law* means "bad money drives out good."

By good money, Gresham meant coinage whose precious-metal content has considerable worth in and of itself, independent of the value stamped on it as a means of exchange. By bad money, he meant the opposite: coins whose material substance has little or no value. According to the law, as money circulates, the good stuff is always driven out by the bad.

To illustrate: Suppose you have two coins, both of which are worth a dollar. One of the coins is made of silver and the other is lead. Although as regulated means of exchange the two coins have identical value, if you melt them down and cash in the

metal, you will get a lot more for the raw silver than you will for the lead. Gresham's Law predicts that the silver coins eventually will disappear from circulation, because they will get melted down for their bullion while the lead will not. In the days before paper money and credit, the law had major economic implications.

As a metaffect, Gresham's Law can be used when anything admirable, precious, or simply worthwhile is made subservient to or eliminated by something of lesser value. The utility of the term is illustrated in this remark from author and radical cultural critic Dwight MacDonald: "There seems to be a Gresham's Law in cultural as well as monetary circulation: bad stuff drives out the good, since it is more easily understood and enjoyed."

Taking MacDonald's lead, the next time you feel like decrying the lack of substance and artistic merit in network television, you can demonstrate that your vocabulary lacks neither substance nor artistic merit: "There must be a Gresham's Law of entertainment; the bad shows always drive out the good, because for some reason junk appeals to larger numbers of people."

Perhaps there is a Gresham's Law of politics as well. With the media and the opposition party hovering around every official like buzzards waiting to pounce on the first sign of impropriety, and with salaries in the private sector far exceeding those in public life, fewer and fewer qualified men and women are willing to run for office. Potential leaders with dignity and dedication to noble ideals are driven out by the venal, the corrupt, the incompetent, and the egomaniacal, who are more than willing to do whatever is necessary to get elected. Make sure this metaffect is near the tip of your tongue when the next election campaign rolls around.

Sports is a natural arena for Gresham's Law. Every true fan knows that when his team loses, it's a case of the bad prevailing over the good due to some lamentable combination of luck, bad officiating, and demons, not to mention deplorable decisions by the team's management. Fans of perennial losers like the Cleveland Indians or the Atlanta Falcons are accustomed to watching good players ship off to other locations while the home-team roster gets freshly stocked with overpriced stiffs. The next time your team announces a player transaction, you can tell your compadres, "Mark my words, it's Gresham's Law all over again. Good players driven out by bad."

One can also postulate a Gresham's Law of the psyche, in which positive thoughts are driven out by the negative, and emotions such as joy, reverence, and love are displaced by anger and despair. If a friend says, "You sound awfully gloomy," your explanation might be, "I'm sorry, when I don't get enough sleep, my nervous system gets greshamed and all these bad feelings drive out the good."

Conversely, when a friend's mood plummets, you might avert further descent by warning, "Think positive. Don't let Gresham's Law get the better of you."

Sir Gresham seemed to have hit on something more useful than he could possibly have imagined when he conceived his law—that is, if he did indeed conceive it. Some historians maintain that the principle to which Gresham's name was attached was, in fact, formulated long before his time. According to this theory, the true originator disappeared from history, driven out somehow by a Johnny-come-lately who became immortal in his stead. Ironically, Gresham himself may have been party to a perverse example of the metaffect that bears his name.

The Haelen Effect

The Anglo-Saxon word *haelen*, meaning "to become whole," is the source of the word *heal*. Therefore, to capture the notion that healing is a natural mechanism by which an ailing organism restores its lost wholeness, Janet F. Quinn coined the term *Haelen Effect*.

Quinn is an associate professor of nursing at the University of South Carolina and a frequent contributor to the literature on alternative health-care practices. Like her colleagues in the holistic health movement, she considers healing "a total, organismic, synergistic response that must emerge from within the individual if recovery and growth are to be accomplished." The Haelen Effect, says Quinn, can be stimulated by any number of methods, from surgery and drugs to caring words and the therapeutic touch. She adds, "The elicitation of the effect, the total organismic response toward wholeness, is the goal of any healing intervention."

In other words, when you are cured of an illness or injury, it is neither the medicine, the hospital's high-tech gadgetry, nor your prayers that does the actual healing. All treatments, remedies, and psychological adjuncts contribute to one common goal: to trigger the Haelen Effect, your body's natural tendency to restore its wholeness. In any given case, one type of treatment might be more effective than another in stimulating the complex, elegant curative processes that nature provided every living being. Therefore, when someone says, "I'm so happy that drug worked for you," the appropriate reply might be, "The medicine as such didn't cure me. It was the Haelen Effect."

The Haelen Effect has interesting implications when you broaden its uses metaffectively. Presumably, the natural urge to wholeness belongs not just to our bodies but to our minds and spirits. Indeed, one could even speculate that it belongs not just to humans but to all of nature's creatures and to all things great and small—from cells to organizations, families to nations, gardens to galaxies. Each unit of creation is probably compelled by a built-in yearning to become whole and moves in that direction naturally.

When you feel stressed out and fragmented and your spirit cries out for a restoration of wholeness, nature might be telling you it's time to rejuvenate yourself. It could be time to tell your boss and your family, "I'm going to a spa for a few days. I need a dose of the Haelen Effect."

The Haelen Effect can also apply to aggregations of people. If some vituperation has ruptured your family's sense of unity, you might gather everyone together and say, "Let's all air our feelings. We need to haelenize this family." If your company falls into chaos because of, say, the sudden death of a leader, you will want to inspire your colleagues to generate an organizational Haelen Effect.

The metaffect can also be applied to whole societies. For example, after an earthquake devastated the San Francisco Bay area in 1989, the whole region needed healing. One might say that resuming the World Series had a haelenizing impact. Historians could say that the Marshall Plan was an ingenious way to kindle the Haelen Effect in war-ravaged Europe. And of our own country, one might say that after the upheaval of Watergate, Gerald Ford was the perfect man to haelenize America.

But let's not lose sight of Janet Quinn's original intention. When someone you care about becomes ill, you can probably do nothing more useful than to remind him of his body's natural tendency to restore wholeness. By helping him draw on his strength and hope, you might actually trigger the Haelen Effect.

The Halo Effect

Around the turn of the century, Thomas Alva Edison was consulted continually on political and philosophical matters. The public was eager to hear his views about everything, figuring that since he was the genius whose inventions were transforming their lives, he must be a wise and learned man. The aura created by Edison's scientific work cast a positive glow on his every thought.

This tendency to judge someone favorably in many areas because of a single salutary characteristic is called by psychologists the *Halo Effect*. First discovered empirically by E. L. Thorndike, an early pioneer in American psychology, the Halo Effect is one of the more common ways we go astray when making judgments about others. Many experiments have proven that when subjects are given positive information about other people, they will rate those individuals highly in characteristics that have nothing to do with what they've been told. In other words, when we do not know enough to form a truly reliable judgment, we infer whether a person is smart or dumb, popular or an outcast, considerate or selfish, humble or arrogant, and so forth by extrapolating from the limited facts we are given.

The metaffective potential of this term is obvious. Today with so few Edisons around, we bestow halos on all kinds of celebrities. The average person probably knows more about the political opinions and personal philosophies of movie stars, talk show hosts, and news anchors than the thoughts of Nobel laureates, Pulitzer Prize winners, or even his locally elected officials.

But the effect does not apply only to celebrities; it influences our judgment of virtually everyone we encounter. The halo of being good-looking, tall, or successful can cast a glow on an entire person, making us think he or she is also honest, generous, or popular. Most people will judge a plain-looking woman in eyeglasses to be more intelligent than a sexy blond woman and assume that the blond is more popular and fun-loving. Indeed, a recent study by political scientist Shawn W. Rosenberg found that by manipulating the photographs of mock candidates for office (changing hairstyles, clothing, and makeup) one could raise or lower their ratings by as much as 20 percent.

The metaffect will come in handy in a number of everyday circumstances. If someone decides to vote for a mayoral candidate just because her dentist endorsed him, you might challenge the decision with, "You're getting caught up in the Halo Effect. He may be great at filling teeth, but what does he know about filling potholes?"

Similarly, if the new boss glad-hands everyone at the company picnic, dressed in jeans and shirt-sleeves and accompanied by a happy, attractive family, he will probably be judged a regular guy who will be fair to his employees. At the risk of being labeled a cynic, you might counsel others to defer judgment: "Don't get carried away by the Halo Effect, folks. Let's see what he's like when he's in that executive suite."

Some people are lucky enough to be the beneficiaries of someone else's halo. Are we not more likely to hire someone if his previous employer was a person of prominence? Are the offspring of respected parents not given opportunities denied the children of anonymities? Don't some married people benefit from their spouses' reputations? Would anyone ask Ed McMahon to endorse their products if millions of people didn't go to sleep having just seen him lit up by Johnny Carson's aura?

As any advertising or public relations expert can testify, halos can be cast over institutions and products as well as individuals. For example, many experts believe that the Ford Motor Company purchased Jaguar just to upgrade its image.

Not just car companies, even countries can acquire halos. Although he did not use the term, author Paul Theroux described in an article how a halo was erected over China. Throughout the 1980s, Kentucky Fried Chicken outlets opened in Beijing, a thousand beauty salons and discos bloomed, and planeloads of industrialists, politicians, and scholars returned with hope and dollar signs in their eyes. We saw all this, and we saw diminutive leader Deng Xiaoping toast the future of his country's ties with the West, and we forgot that between 1983 and 1986, Deng's government had executed 10,000 people without benefit of due process. Then came June 3, 1989, and the halo that had hovered over China disintegrated at Tiananmen Square.

Naturally, there is a converse to the Halo Effect: the *Devil Effect*. People or institutions can also be judged negatively solely on the basis of one characteristic, however irrelevant. According to Ralph Keyes, author of *The Height of Your Life*, short people earn about $500 per inch less each year than their taller counterparts. Many executives carry around their old school loyalties to the point where they won't hire anyone who graduated from a rival institution. And in some circles, you can be deviled if you don't wear Gucci, Pucci, or whatever.

That sartorial Devil's Effect is more insidious than amusing: it is affecting children in a frightening way. According to school officials and psychologists, brand-name garments have become badges of honor among youngsters. Says the *Los Angeles Times*: "Show up for school without them, students say, and they may be ridiculed, scorned and sometimes even ostracized by their classmates."

So keep both variations of this metaffect in mind when making critical judgments, lest you trip over a luminous ring or a cloven hoof.

Heisenberg's Uncertainty Principle

In the United States, the 1920s roared with flappers and bootleg gin and larger-than-life heroes such as Babe Ruth, Jack Dempsey, and Charles Lindbergh. In Germany, the roar was more cerebral and subversive. The Bauhaus school was revolutionizing art and architecture; Carl Jung and Alfred Adler were taking Freud's work in new directions; Bertolt Brecht was transforming theater, and the Dadaists were attacking conventional esthetic standards with calculated absurdity and the veneration of spontaneity. In the universities, a group of youngsters jolted the underpinnings of modern science by engaging in what has been called "Dada physics."

Among the revolutionaries was a young man named Werner Heisenberg. In 1927, at the age of twenty-six, Heisenberg formulated a theory that would earn him a place beside Albert Einstein, Niels Bohr, and other scientific giants whose impact continues to restructure the way we look at the world.

In simple terms, this is what Heisenberg discovered: one can determine the position of a subatomic particle, and one can calculate the velocity of that particle, but one cannot do both simultaneously. The reason for this is astonishingly simple: in and of itself, the process of making either kind of observation (determining position or velocity) alters the very conditions you are observing. The more accurately you measure location, the less accurately you can measure speed, and vice versa. The very presence of an observer means that one variable or the other will always remain shrouded in uncertainty.

Heisenberg's Uncertainty Principle exposed a fundamental, inescapable property of the universe: the act of observation changes what you are observing. For science, this was profoundly disturbing. "The fundamental importance of the uncertainty principle," writes Fritjof Capra in *The Tao of Physics,* "is that it expresses the limitations of our classical concepts in a precise mathematical form. . . . Our classical notions, derived from our ordinary macroscopic experience, are not fully adequate to describe this world." This meant that science would never attain its cherished ideal: to construct a model of the universe in which one could, by calculating present conditions, predict future events with perfect accuracy. Predictions about subatomic events now had to be expressed as probabilities, not certainties.

A major milestone in Western thought, the Uncertainty Principle belies the notion that human beings can be totally detached, objective observers, able to poke and probe nature without altering it. As one physicist put it, to observe is to disturb. "Natural science," said Heisenberg, "does not simply describe and explain nature; it is part of the interplay between nature and ourselves. . . . What we observe is not nature itself, but nature exposed to our method of questioning."

That last sentence brings the principle home to all of us and suggests its metaffective implication: it is not just the location and velocity of atoms that defy exact description; all life as we know it is a reflection, not of some pristine reality "out there" but of reality *as we see it.* Our very presence influences what we know . . . or think we know.

Viewed in a negative light, the Uncertainty Principle can generate a kind of existential despair over the futility of trying to be certain about anything. It casts a pall over big things, like self-knowledge (can we ever be certain of who we are?) as well as over little things, like our perception of daily events (do the funny things on TV's "Candid Camera" happen only because the cameras are watching?).

Where interpersonal relationships are concerned, the principle suggests that familiarity breeds uncertainty, not contempt. Think of it this way: if we can't possibly know whether what we know would be so if we were not there knowing it, how can we ever truly know another human being? For instance, are your kids behaving themselves because they know you are watching them, or would they be perfect angels anyway? Can you really predict what your spouse will be like in the future, given that what he or she becomes will be influenced by your presence?

At work, is the customer service department always that efficient, or were they tipped off that you were keeping an eye on them? (Maybe you'd better plant video cameras instead—

and how will that affect what you see?) Does the sales staff treat customers too politely when no executives are around? (Maybe you should bug the showroom.)

Taking a more positive stance, knowing that uncertainty is part of the human condition enables one to be more stoic in the face of life's conundrums. For example, you think you have someone pegged because you've known him and his family for years, but then he does something contrary to your expectations: "I don't know what to make of the guy. Oh, well, I should have known better. You can't negate the Uncertainty Principle."

The principle might also make you more skeptical in the best sense of the word—less likely to be duped. Suppose you are given the results of some market research. Rather than accept it at face value, you can demand, "How do you know this isn't tarnished by Heisenberg's Uncertainty Principle? Maybe the subjects changed their minds because of how you asked the questions, and now they'll change them back again."

In a more mundane example, the next time you are tempted to go to an expensive restaurant because it received an enthusiastic review, remember what Jonathan Gold of the *Los Angeles Times* called the Heisenberg's Uncertainty Principle of Food Criticism: "You can't review a restaurant without altering its nature." Perhaps four-star reviews ought to be taken with a grain of salt.

Of course, if you're not careful, overusing this metaffect can make you sound like an inveterate cynic. Suppose you leave a party and your wife innocently remarks, "Aren't the Andersons wonderful? They seem so happy together." If you find yourself thinking, "How can you be certain they're not happy only when there are people around?" you might want to hold your tongue.

Perhaps the most humbling aspect of the Uncertainty Principle is this: of all the things we want to know, the one we want *most* to know perfectly is ourselves—and that is probably the one object of knowledge most affected by the principle. How can we know ourselves without altering ourselves? How can we even think about ourselves without knowing we are thinking about ourselves and therefore changing how we think about ourselves?

Contemplate such matters too much and you'll end up in a wonderland of either befuddlement or enlightenment. But how will you know for certain which state you're in?

Hubble's Law

The universe is running away from us. Every star, every galaxy, every cluster of galaxies—all things twinkling in the velvet night and all those beyond the range of our eyes and our telescopes are hurtling away from us at unimaginable speed.

But don't take it personally. The heavenly bodies have nothing against earth. Any creature in any galaxy would notice the same phenomenon: everything is running away. In fact, the stars and galaxies are all flying away from one another, and the distance between them gets greater and greater by the second.

The dynamics of this galactic diaspora are described by *Hubble's Law*. It was named for the American astronomer Edwin Powell Hubble, who first recognized it in 1929 when he observed that the light emanating from distant galaxies was systematically shifting toward the red end of the spectrum. As explained by the Doppler Effect (see page 76), this "red shift" means the galaxies are moving away from us. Hubble noted

two other things: the more distant the galaxy, the faster it
recedes; and the gaps between the galaxies are getting bigger
all the time. This was the first evidence that the universe is
expanding and a crucial factor in convincing scientists that the
cosmos began with a big bang billions of years ago.

The next time you're gazing up at the canopy of night, you
can reflect on the mind-boggling notion that the sparkling
lights that seem to be suspended like crystals in a chandelier
are actually hurtling away from one another and us at speeds

of up to 17,000 miles per second. If you have a companion you want to impress, explain how this was discovered, and add, "The spectral red shift of the receding galaxies is proportional to the speed of the recession and the distance from us. That's Hubble's Law." That should win you a few stars.

But why restrict a good principle to the purpose for which it was intended? Metaffectively, many things fly faster and faster away as time and distance increase, such as old friends or former lovers. As they recede from your awareness, the psychic and emotional ties that once bound you to each other seem to pull you apart with increasing strength: "We used to be so close, but we were hubbled by time. As the years passed, we grew farther and farther apart, and now it's as though we're in different galaxies."

The term is also appropriate for those times when a small difference of opinion comes between two people and their points of view start flying apart with intergalactic speed, racing farther from any common ground as time goes by. When that happens, you might urge, "Let's start the retro rockets and slow this argument down before Hubble's Law pulls us so far apart we won't be able to hear each other."

Lies and rumors probably expand according to some analog of Hubble's Law. Have you noticed how a tiny falsehood or the wispiest whisper through the grapevine can take off and fly out of hand so quickly that its proximity to the truth gets more and more distant with each repetition? If you find yourself in such a situation, try this: "My God, Hubble's Law has run amuck! I can't locate a speck of truth in this galaxy of rumors even with a telescope."

The metaffect is also a good way to describe what often happens to memories. As time goes by, events seem to recede at an ever-quickening pace from the mind's retrieval mechanism. Our recollections often seem to hurtle away until they seem as disconnected from us and one another as distant stars.

You may someday be reminiscing with an old friend about bygone days, when your conversation starts to sound like the duet between Maurice Chevalier and Hermione Gingold in *Gigi:*

"We met at nine."

"We met at eight."

"I was on time."

"No, you were late."

"Ah yes, I remember it well."

After you laugh together and warmly sigh about how fickle the flickering of memory can be, you can impress your friend by mentioning this metaffect. And you can sparkle further by making a pun on it: "Watching your memories fly away is a hubbling experience."

That is, if you don't forget this metaffect about forgetting.

The Isaac Complex

"Take now thy son, thine only son Isaac, whom thou lovest, and get thee unto the land of Moriah; and offer him there for a burnt offering upon one of the mountains which I will tell thee of."

So said God to Abraham, and Abraham followed the sacred orders to the letter. "And they came to the place which God had told him of; and Abraham built an altar there, and laid the wood in order, and bound Isaac his son, and laid him on the altar upon the wood. And Abraham stretched forth his hand, and took the knife to slay his son."

We all know what happened: God stayed Abraham's hand. It

was essentially a test, and the patriarch passed with flying colors. Because he was willing to sacrifice his beloved son, Abraham was blessed handsomely and his seed multiplied "as the stars of the heaven."

Most commentators and clerics have interpreted the tale from the point of view of Abraham, as a testament to the power of faith and the advantages of obeying divine will. But what about little Isaac? Is there a lesson in the story if we look at it from the perspective of a young boy trembling before his own father's knife? Erich Neumann thought so. A psychologist who studied with Carl Jung in the 1930s, Neumann used the term *Isaac Complex* to refer to what he called "patriarchal castration."

In *The Origins and History of Consciousness,* Neumann describes the characteristic symptom of the complex: "Isaac's utter reliance upon his father, whom he follows in all things without ever standing on his own feet." In other words, the Isaac Complex entails inordinate respect for authority, the result of which is a kind of impotence, a stifling of one's own inner voice in favor of conformity to patriarchal rule. This, says Neumann, leads to a "sterile conservatism and a reactionary identification with the father."

If one accepts Neumann's reading of the biblical tale, the term Isaac Complex might be used to describe those personalities who, like Isaac yielding his breath to his father's hand, surrender their individuality and power of choice to the authority of another human being, an organization, an ideology, a code of behavior, or a symbol such as a flag, an emblem, or a uniform. Included among such Isaacs would be sticklers for orthodoxy, whether religious, political, or otherwise; fanatical, unthinking ideologues of all stripes; rigid, frightened souls who hide behind inflexible rules; true believers who blindly follow leaders, and soldiers who march like lemmings to their doom without questioning their orders.

As an everyday manifestation, the metaffect could be applied to a college student who becomes so enthralled by a professor's wisdom that he quotes him at every opportunity. You might tell the would-be acolyte, "I'm sure Doctor Smart is a brilliant scholar, but a prophet he's not. Think for yourself or you'll end up with an Isaac Complex."

The next time a government official comes under investigation for a suspected misdeed and his attorney claims he was only following orders, you might take this position: "Maybe he did think he was acting in the best interests of the country. Maybe he was ordered to do it. But the law is the law and the Isaac Complex is not a valid defense."

Some other examples:

"She never should have put all her career aspirations in that guy's hands. She isaaced herself into a dead end."

"I know you trust your doctor, but get a second opinion anyway. There's a fine line between trust and the Isaac Complex."

"I don't think we should force our own views on little Albert. If he doesn't learn to make his own decisions, he'll end up with an Isaac Complex."

"Look, I don't want to be sacrificed on the altar of the IRS. Lose this Isaac Complex of yours, or I'll find an accountant who's a little more creative."

A woman I once met had suffered financial ruin and a great deal of humiliation because of the Isaac Complex. Enchanted by a new guru, she ended up becoming the most favored of his handful of disciples, an honor that entailed freely dispensing offerings of sex and money. Unfortunately, no one was around to say, "Lose this charlatan now, before he isaacs you out of your inheritance and your self-respect," for that is just what happened.

Then again, the guru might have won her over by giving the Isaac story a different spin. Clearly, the authors of the Bible saw

Abraham's son as virtuous, a symbol of a love so pure and a trust so complete that he was willing to make the ultimate sacrifice if his father so wished. After all, God rewarded Isaac handsomely for his act of surrender. Spared by divine intervention, the lad grew up to be rich in land and possessions. He married Rebecca and fathered Jacob and Esau and lived the longest of all the patriarchs.

It is, however, the negative side for which Neumann named the complex. If the metaffect catches on, it can stand as a potent warning against the stultifying consequences of blind conformity: "Beware of the Isaac Complex, youngsters. Hold fast to your individuality."

❦

Janiger's Law

One of the metaffects with which most of us are familiar is the Peter Principle, which states that people rise to the level of their own incompetence. It was invented by Lawrence Peter to explain the commonly observed phenomenon in which people are promoted to managerial positions because of their excellent performance in, say, sales or research. The problem is, a crack salesman doesn't necessarily make a good executive, an outstanding scientist doesn't necessarily shine when asked to administer a large research operation, a terrific shortstop does not automatically turn into Casey Stengel if given a shot at managing, and an inspiring teacher may not cut the mustard as a department head or school principal. They are, as Peter put it, promoted to the level of their own incompetence.

Since Peter's concept caught on, many people have come up with their own variations of it. Management consultant Christopher Hegarty, for example, developed Hegarty's Leadership Heresy, which states that people rise to the level of their boss's ignorance. Managers often promote people for the wrong reasons, Hegarty believes, assessing incorrectly their qualifications and training.

Psychiatrist Oscar Janiger has another variation: people rise to the level of their own anxieties. Janiger, who conducted groundbreaking research on psychoactive drugs and taught psychiatry at leading medical schools, derived *Janiger's Law* from forty years of clinical experience. "The person reaches a threshold at which he calculates that playing the game is no longer worth it," says Janiger. "It happens when they come in contact with situations that bring up frightening psychological issues. Rationally, they might want to forge ahead, but if the anxiety is strong enough, they'll determine they can't go on. They've reached the limit."

According to Janiger, when a situation arises that resembles conditions the person has previously encountered, he makes an estimate based on a sort of internal anxiety meter that tells him whether his threshold of tolerance has been reached. If the earlier experience caused anxiety, the next time he will tend to err on the cautious side, stopping short of the threshold to protect himself from going through the anxiety once again.

Janiger emphasizes that the law has nothing to do with our actual capacities. We apply the brakes to ourselves not because we lack the ability to accomplish the job, but because we're afraid of something: the fear of failure, or embarrassment, or whatever manifests as anxiety. Soon we come to fear the anxiety itself. We stop ourselves well before we reach our actual capacity, at a place where we *think* or *fear* that we can't function. Instead of obeying the proverb "A man's reach should exceed his grasp," we might list toward another one: "Don't bite off more than you can chew" or, more accurately, don't take on more than your nervous system can handle.

Say you are rising on the corporate ladder and are offered a promotion or a golden opportunity to demonstrate your abilities. Suddenly, your confidence is shattered. You tremble at the prospect of having more responsibility. Your mind comes up with a dozen reasons why turning down the promotion, or ignoring the opportunity, would be sensible and prudent and, in fact, a superior strategy in the long run. If you want to break through the anxiety, you'd better hope that your inner voice reminds you of this metaffect: "Don't back down. You're falling victim to Janiger's Law."

The concept is not limited to professional advancement, of course. Suppose there's someone you want to meet. He or she is attractive, intelligent, interesting, and manifestly desirable. Your mind hedges: "In the past, starting a conversation with such a person has always triggered a rush of anxiety. Instead, why not talk to that nice, ordinary person over there?" Perhaps now you will have the wherewithal to respond, "I'm sick of taking the less threatening road. I am hereby revoking Janiger's Law."

Faced with a Janiger situation, you have a choice. You can opt out—that is, yield to the anxiety and turn down the challenge—in which case the anxiety threshold will stay where it is, or perhaps get even lower. Or you can persevere, muddle through, accept the challenge, and do your best to manage the anxiety. By so doing, you might raise the ceiling of anxiety for the next occasion, thereby making progress. The latter is the equivalent of getting right back on the bicycle after you've taken a spill.

So, if you've been turning down invitations to beach parties rather than wear a swimsuit in front of your new friends, if you're running out of excuses for not making that speech, if you're not returning calls from the company that wants to interview you, if you've run out of phone calls to make and dishes to wash and pencils to sharpen while your novel-in-progress beckons from a file drawer, you might want to post a reminder on your refrigerator: "Beware of Janiger's Law."

The Jonah Complex

Most people remember Jonah as the unfortunate guy who got swallowed by a whale in the Bible story. What they probably don't remember is the decision that got him into that mess. It started when God said to him, "Arise, go to Ninevah, that great city, and cry against it; for their wickedness is come up before me."

But Jonah, overwhelmed by the magnitude of the Lord's entreaty, deserted his mission. He took off and fled for Tarshish by boat. When a mighty tempest threatened to destroy the ship, the other passengers tossed Jonah overboard, because they believed it was his disobedience that had caused the Lord to visit his wrath upon the sea. That's when Jonah was swallowed by the great fish.

The story is usually viewed as an allegory supporting the wisdom of submitting to divine imperatives. However, the great pioneering psychologist Abraham Maslow saw it differently. Maslow—who did a Fosbury Flop (see page 93) on the discipline of psychology by focusing on the highest and brightest potential of humans instead of the dark and dingy recesses of the subconscious—identified an affliction he characterized as "an escape from greatness." He named this refusal to face up to one's capacities and change one's world the *Jonah Complex*. Warned Maslow, "If you deliberately set out to be less than you are capable, you'll be unhappy for the rest of your life."

We all know underachievers. We all know talented, intellegent people who don't live up to their promise. We all know people who shy away from responsibility or find ways to sabotage their own endeavors just before they achieve success. If Maslow was right about the extraordinary potential we possess for accomplishment, joy, and fulfillment, then we owe it to ourselves to face up to our own jonahesque tendencies. For example: "So what if I'm forty. I've been putting off what I really want to do for years. I'm not going to jonah myself any longer."

We also owe it to others to warn them against jonahesque behavior. Someone who clamps down on the expression of a talent, or shies away from a challenge, or refuses to obey a sense of calling ought to be cautioned, "Don't succumb to the Jonah Complex, or you'll get tossed into a sea of misery and swallowed by the great fish of regret."

Parents, teachers, and indeed anyone in a mentor or supervisory position will no doubt find opportunities to use this metaffect. For example:

"Sally could be better than a C student if she'd only get over her Jonah Complex."

"Management has to be less intimidating. They've jonahed that whole division into mediocrity."

The biblical tale is a reminder that it's never too late to reverse the escape from greatness. Jonah remained in the belly of the beast for three days, praying and offering up earnest apologies and supplications to God. When God was satisfied that the captive prophet had learned his lesson, he ordered the fish to vomit him up. Given another chance, Jonah did his job, preaching to the people of Ninevah with such skill and conviction that they did as he said. "And God saw their works, that they turned from their evil way; and God repented of the evil that he had said that he would do unto them; and he did it not."

We all have greatness in us, Maslow's work informs us. If we tap into it we can transform ourselves, and possibly our small corners of the world as well. The human tragedy is in failing to live up to our potential. Perhaps the eleventh commandment should be "Thou shalt not capitulate to the Jonah Complex."

The Lake Wobegon Effect

When John J. Cannell, a physician living in West Virginia, wanted to know about the quality of schools in the state, he queried education officials in every district. To a person, they informed him that the students in their own areas scored above the national average on standardized achievement tests. This surprised Dr. Cannell, because West Virginia was not exactly famous for the quality of its schools: it had the third-lowest college entrance scores in the country, the second-highest percentage of adults without a college education, and the second-lowest per capita income. Intrigued by the incongruity, Dr. Cannell spent $11,000 of his own money to do something no one had done before: survey test scores on a national basis.

Dr. Cannell's nonprofit group, Friends for Education, sent letters to superintendents and testing coordinators in all fifty states. What they learned caused an uproar in educational circles: at the elementary level, it seemed, every state scored above the "national norm" on standardized tests—even states that ranked dreadfully low on graduation rates, college entrance exam scores, and literacy.

How can virtually every child be above average? They can't. Not unless they live in Lake Wobegon, Minnesota, the mythological town that humorist Garrison Keillor immortalized on his radio program, "A Prairie Home Companion." In Lake Wobegon, as Keillor would inform his weekly audience, "all the women are strong, all the men are good-looking, and all the children are above average." For that reason, when Dr. Cannell made public the results of his survey, outraged officials at the U.S. Department of Education dubbed the misleading data the *Lake Wobegon Effect.*

The reason that school officials could get away with inflating the significance of the scores is this: when students take a standardized test, their scores are not compared with those of their contemporaries, but with those of a "norm group" who may have taken the exam as many as ten years earlier, when the test was new. Furthermore, since school districts have a vested interest in their students' scores, they typically gear their curricula to the content of the tests and prepare their pupils to respond properly to those questions. Hence, the scores invariably improve over time, which gives school systems a chance to gloat about their "above-average" students. Cannell points out that only three states administer exams in such a way that teachers cannot deliberately prepare students for them; in those states, the improvement in scores is way below that of all the others.

The Lake Wobegon Effect is about the treachery of statistics. As a metaffect, it can be applied to deceptive facts of all kinds. We are constantly bombarded with statistical terminology from advertisers, health advisers, politicians, reporters, sports announcers, salespeople, et al., and we are easily bamboozled, because most of us are relatively unschooled about this arcane discipline. Normally, it takes a sophisticated whistle-blower like Dr. Cannell to scratch the surface of statistical gloss and reveal the blemishes beneath. However, having the Lake Wobegon Effect in your lexicon of metaffects might help you spot statistical hokum when you see it.

For example, suppose a sales manager gets up before your executive committee and states, "I am proud to report that 60 percent of our sales force improved their records over last year's performance." Afterward, you can inform your colleagues: "He tried to pull the Lake Wobegon Effect over our eyes. What he didn't say was that two of every five salespeople did *worse* than last year. The question is, how *much* worse."

Or suppose you're trying to lose weight, and the promoter of a dietary supplement tells you that 80 percent of the people who have used her product lost an average of ten pounds. You might ask how many dieters the survey consisted of and exactly how much weight each of them lost. Perhaps five people were questioned and one gained three pounds, three lost six pounds each, and one miraculously lost twenty-five. Your conclusion: "Get lost before I call the Lake Wobegon patrol."

Suppose you and your spouse are looking for a financial adviser. You meet with one who boasts, "Half my clients double their investments within three years." If you don't want your savings to sink in Lake Wobegon, grab your spouse's hand before he signs on the dotted line and ask about the *other* half, the ones who *don't* double their money.

In a larger metaffective sense, the Lake Wobegon Effect is about overstatement for the purpose of puffing up pride. Boasts such as "We're the best," whether applied to schools, companies, or towns, smack of Lake Wobegon fever. If you ever have to sit through a high-powered motivational speech marked by statements like "You are part of the world's greatest carpet-cleaning company," you can excuse yourself with "Yeah, and all the women are strong and the men good-looking."

If use of this metaffect spreads, there's a chance we can get rid of many Lake Wobegonlike claims that surround us, such as TV commercials that claim that nine out of ten doctors recommend their product and those silly giant fingers at sports events that say "We're number 1."

The McNaughton Rule

On January 20, 1843, Edward Drummond, the private secretary of Prime Minister Sir Robert Peel, was walking near Charing Cross in London on his way home when he was shot in the back at point-blank range. The assassin, a thirty-year-old woodturner named Daniel McNaughton, calmly placed the weapon in his coat pocket and drew a second pistol. However, McNaughton had chosen an inappropriate time and place to commit his heinous deed. It was broad daylight on a busy thoroughfare, and a policeman was standing close enough to grab the culprit's arm and knock him to the ground before he could fire another shot. That was not McNaughton's only mistake: he had actually intended to kill the prime minister, whom the unfortunate Drummond happened to resemble.

Five days later, the victim died from the one shot McNaughton managed to fire. The assailant's trial at Old Bailey was not only a media sensation at the time but also set a binding legal precedent in England and the United States for almost a century. The *McNaughton Rule* established new criteria for insanity centered on the knowledge of right and wrong.

In a pattern that has by now become familiar, McNaughton's defense pleaded innocent by reason of insanity. Strengthened by the testimony of physicians, his attorneys painted a convincing portrait of lunacy. They told how the defendant had sold the modest family business he'd inherited because he thought "spies" were following him day and night. They said he had tried to protest this "persecution" to government officials, since he blamed it on the Tory Party. They revealed that, a few months before the murder, McNaughton had been evicted from his lodgings because fellow tenants complained about his loud moans and mutterings—reactions to the spies that were prowling his bedroom and the atrocious lies about him that were cleverly concealed in newspapers. They pointed out that he was sleeping in open fields when he decided that he could obtain peace of mind only by bumping off the leader of the Tories.

The prosecution, on the other hand, tried to demonstrate that McNaughton was actually quite sane and had acted rationally when planning the murder, despite the mistaken identity and the ridiculous choice of time and place. According to Thomas W. Maeder's *Crime and Madness,* a history of the insanity defense, witnesses testified that the defendant seemed a harmless, inoffensive fellow, mild and reasonable in his behavior, who loved to feed birds and watch children at play. In other words, he was as sane as you or me.

In the end, Daniel McNaughton was declared insane and committed to a lunatic asylum. The acquittal prompted cries of outrage from common citizens, newspapers, and dignitaries. Queen Victoria herself objected to the verdict on legal and moral grounds and, in a whimsical moment, on political grounds as well; she felt that anyone who wanted to kill a Tory Prime Minister could not be considered all that crazy.

Subsequent to the trial, the issue of insanity was hotly debated in the House of Lords until legislators and jurists settled

on the test that would become known as the McNaughton Rule: "To establish a defence on the ground of insanity, it must be clearly proved that, at the time of the committing of the act, the party accused was labouring under such a defect of reason, from disease of the mind, as not to know the nature and quality of the act he was doing; or if he did know it, that he did not know that he was doing what was wrong."

While the advent of modern psychiatry has changed the way the law treats the insanity plea, the McNaughton Rule might be used by anyone outside of a courtroom as a metaffective defense for regrettable behavior: "I'm really sorry I had a temper tantrum [kicked the dog, told the boss to stuff the job, spent the rent money on a new wardrobe, etc.]; however, I wish to be pardoned by virtue of the McNaughton Rule. At the time I did it, my mind was diseased. I did not know the nature and quality of my action. And I certainly didn't know it was wrong."

In fact, you could strengthen your case by blaming your transgression on something that temporarily disturbed the electrochemical balance of your brain: high-power lines, perhaps, or fumes from a nearby smokestack. It could even be something you ate—as in the infamous "Twinkie Defense," which got Dan White, slayer of San Francisco Mayor George Moscone and Supervisor Harvey Milk, a sentence so light that it sparked a riot. "Gee, officer, did I really run that red light? It must have been those damn donuts. The sugar McNaughtoned my brain."

The Meissner Effect

If you start an electric current going in a ring of ordinary metal, it will die out fairly quickly due to the electrical resistance caused by the chaotic motion of electrons. As certain metals get colder, however, they become more conductive, less resistant to current. If you make these metals cold enough—*extremely* cold, just a few degrees above absolute zero (minus 459 degrees Fahrenheit)—they become, quite abruptly, *superconductors.* Start an electric current in a loop of superconductive metal and it will persist virtually forever, undiminished. The resistance is zero because, at that temperature, the electrons function as one coherent whole, lined up like soldiers in perfect step.

One of the more remarkable characteristics of superconductors is the *Meissner Effect,* discovered by the German physicists W. Meissner and R. Ochsenfeld in 1933. (No, I don't know why this phenomenon is called the *Meissner Effect,* not the Meissner-Ochsenfeld Effect.) Ordinarily, if you place a metal in an electromagnetic field, it will become totally permeated by that field; that is, the electromagnetism will not only surround the metal but will penetrate it, much as water both surrounds and penetrates a sponge dropped into a sink. If a superconducting metal is cooled toward the critical temperature, however, it dispels the magnetic field from within itself. Ultimately, when it reaches full superconductor status, the metal is liberated; the magnetic field flows around it like a stream of water around a rock, but it does not penetrate.

Metaffectively speaking, the Meissner Effect can also refer to the psychophysiology of humans. As physicist Lawrence P. Domash has suggested, lowering the temperature of a metal is similar to calming down a human nervous system through techniques like yogic meditation. Just as the molecules in a cooled object become less active and more orderly, presumably, so does the brain of a mystic. If he achieves the state of perfect stillness and absence of thought known in India as *samadhi,* the adept becomes like a superconductor, tuned in to the infinite currents of the universe much as the analogous metal eternally conducts currents of electricity.

According to yogic texts, the achievement of *samadhi* induces a state of such impermeable equanimity that the adept is compared to "a candle in a windless place." Suffused by bliss, undiminished by sorrow or joy, loss or gain, the adept's state of consciousness creates a kind of spiritual Meissner Effect; the slings and arrows of outrageous fortune slide off his enlightened back like electromagnetic waves off a super-cooled metal.

To take the metaffect one step farther, if a metal is impure, the Meissner Effect will be only partial: the magnetic field will be able to penetrate some areas and the conductivity will be less than infinite. However, if you remove from the metal all its chemical impurities and physical imperfections, the Meissner Effect will be total. This is reminiscent of yogic injunctions to purify the body and mind lest the benefits of spiritual practice be partial and the bliss merely temporary. The imperfections in superconductive metals are like the *samskaras* in the mind— impressions etched by thoughts and actions that keep the seeker imprisoned by the past and ignorant of the true nature of reality.

If you're not into mysticism, consider the metaffect's wider applications with respect to everyday composure. Think of those times when you wish you had perfect self-possession and durable inner contentment, so that neither loss nor gain, joy nor sorrow could penetrate a millionth of an inch of your psychic well-being. Think of those times when you wished you were imperturbable, so self-assured and self-contained that nothing—not sticks, stones, slaps, or slurs—could make you blow your cool.

While "cool" is a fine word to describe a condition so reminiscent of a superconductor, it has gotten rather stale with use. The Meissner Effect is a fresh alternative. Recalling it might help you in difficult circumstances. If you're under pressure—in a traffic jam with your plane about to take off, facing a rapidly encroaching deadline at work, dealing with a family emergency—you'll want to take a deep breath and tell yourself, "Don't let it get to you. Try to meissner the situation."

If the metaffect catches on, you might one day hear a sportscaster say, "There's no time on the clock. If he sinks this foul shot, the Lakers win the championship. The crowd at Boston Garden is on their feet, screaming and trying to shake him up, but Magic's got the Meissner Effect. The pressure rolls off him like an electromagnetic field off a superconductor."

Or, as you leave a movie theater, you might hear someone marvel at the star: "Man, that Clint Eastwood is one cool dude. He's a walking Meissner Effect."

The Minimax Principle

Bob runs his own small company. He is certain that his competitors are one step ahead of him and up to dirty tricks that will ruin the firm if he is not vigilant. He approaches every business deal as if the negotiator on the other side of the table were privy to secret information and were so cunning and adroit he could run the CIA. Bob makes cost projections and sales estimates as if all the forces of supply and demand were conspiring against his little company. Consistent with his vision of an essentially unfriendly world, he makes defensive decisions, intended to minimize the downside rather than maximize the up. Bob does not know it, but he is operating according to the *Minimax Principle*.

According to psychologists, the usual way we go about making rational decisions is to predict the likely outcome of each possible action and then select the one that stands to maximize our chances of obtaining a desirable result. But the Minimax Principle suggests a slightly different approach. Abraham Wald, the principal architect of statistical decision-making theory back in the 1930s, proposed using it to select the optimum strategy when many strategies are available.

Utilizing the Minimax Principle, you assume that nature as a whole is malevolent and that conditions will come together to create the maximum loss for whichever strategy you select. Consequently, you choose the strategy for which the maximum loss will be as little as possible. In other words, the principle has to do with assuming the worst; minimax means trying to minimize the maximum loss.

I'm not suggesting that you should adopt this metaffect as a worldview; it is likely to turn you into a paranoid misanthrope. However, it can be wisely used as an isolated strategy, an appropriate response to certain conditions. Suppose you are playing what you thought was a polite set of tennis doubles when you realize that your opponents not only want to win but to humiliate you by playing the game with ruthless perfection. You might want to tell your partner, "Okay, we're dealing with formidable foes with malicious intentions. From now on, we're playing by the Minimax Principle. Show no mercy."

People in large cities might plan their evening out using this metaffect: "Hi, Alice. Listen, today let's go by the Minimax Principle. Let's assume that traffic will be at its maximum worst and take the route that's likely to have the minimum congestion. I'd enjoy a drive in the country."

Of course, adopting the Minimax Principle can be dangerous. It is as unwise to overestimate your adversaries as it is to underestimate them. If you assume they are operating with maximum skill, information, resources, and genius, you might overspend to compensate for their supposed superiority, or think their stupid mistakes are actually shrewd strategic maneuvers, or outsmart yourself because you think they know something you don't. By thinking a competitor will stop at nothing to ruin you, you can adopt an overly defensive posture.

Minimaxing also contains the danger of creating a self-fulfilling prophecy. If you gear your strategy to minimizing losses, you might succeed only to end up barely scraping by. You minimize not only your losses but your gains, and that's no way to maximize your potential. If you see an overly bleak outlook taking hold and influencing decisions, call it by name and put a stop to it. "Let's rethink our assumptions before we get sucked into a whirlpool of minimaxing."

So, if you work for a boss like Bob, you might do your company a favor by telling him, "Look, Mister Worst-case Scenario, this company has great potential, but we can't fulfill it if we make every decision according to the Minimax Principle."

As it turns out, the Minimax criteria for decision-making

proved too pessimistic even for statisticians. In 1944, two psychologists named von Neumann and Morganstern published a book called *The Theory of Games and Economic Behavior*. It was an epochal work that altered the way research on decision-making was done, but one aspect of their thesis proved far less fruitful than the rest: the authors' theory depended on the Minimax assumption that one's opponents can play the game with optimal skill. This was rejected as overly conservative; in real life, it was argued, opponents and competitors function ineptly far more often than they do optimally.

Somewhere between panglossian optimism and the bleakness of the Minimax Principle is a realistic vision that recognizes that life is neither a rose garden nor an evil conspiracy. Pragmatic questions aside, who wants to go through life believing that the environment is malevolent, that the odds are stacked against you, and that all your potential competitors are equipped with powers you don't have? With such an outlook, you might as well join those doleful madmen with "The World Is Ending" signs.

Instead, you can get more attention, and perhaps do the world some good, by designing a placard of your own: "God Does Not Believe in the Minimax Principle."

The Moat Effect

If you shine a spot of light on the retina of an animal, the light will stimulate a small area of neuronal activity in the brain. That region, in turn, will be surrounded by an area in which the firing of neurons is inhibited.

Neurophysiologists say this same pattern exists throughout the nervous system: stimulate a small area of the cortex and the surrounding regions will be inhibited. A diagram of this might show a column in the center representing a raised level of activity and a ring of depressed activity surrounding it, like a moat. Dr. John Lilly calls this the *Moat Effect.*

John Lilly is a neuroscientist best known for his pioneering work with dolphins and for mapping the pain and pleasure centers of the brain. In his book *The Dyadic Cyclone,* he also recognized the metaffective potential of the Moat Effect: "I have noticed that in general people tend to do exactly this kind of operation in regard to their knowledge about any given subject. They tend to raise the importance of their own knowledge (make a central column of high importance) and demean areas of knowledge not within their own area of competence (surround it with a moat in regard to other knowledge or other people's knowledge). So the 'moat effect' exists not only in our own neurophysiology, but also in our thought and our behavior and our social activities."

The Moat Effect might well be a universal human trait. In its extreme form, we observe it consistently in know-it-alls and narrow-minded, self-righteous zealots. But, to one degree or another, most of us erect castles of our beliefs and surround them with moats of disinterest, disbelief, and distrust. When we are not stimulated by something, it can be hard to see why anyone else would be.

Lilly points out that the Moat Effect is rampant in politics, wherein candidates "take their own program and their own thinking as if it is the most important thing in the world, and surround it with an area of demeaning other people's programs, opinions and activities."

You can also find deep moats in science and academia, where an individual scientist or scholar might elevate the significance of his particular research and diminish the value of the work of his peers. Indeed, we all can find castles and moats in our offices, living rooms, bars, classrooms, and boardrooms.

Lilly believes that the basic structure of the Moat Effect is built into the wiring of our brains, but if we are conscious of it we can turn the trait into something more positive. He therefore recommends lifting the entire terrain of the mind by raising the base of one's awareness. The result will still be a central peak (the castle of our own beliefs), but the heightened awareness raises the level of the moat so that contrasting viewpoints are not below ground.

In addition to its use as a tool for personal growth, the metaffect will no doubt come in handy whenever you encounter fanatics or pompous, self-important pedants whose minds are closed to anyone else's perspective. Now you have a unique way to let them know you see through them: "I'm out of here. I can't have a civilized discussion with a walking Moat Effect. You've dug a ditch around your own point of view and I can't swim past the crocodiles."

Remembering the metaffect can serve as an antidote to one's own tendency toward narrow-mindedness. The next time you find yourself unwilling to listen to someone else's political views, or disdaining your brother's stamp collection or your sister-in-law's passion for decorated fingernails, ask yourself whether you've fallen prey to the Moat Effect. You might have built your castle on a foundation of sand.

And if someone disdains your favorite undertaking, you might suggest that moats work both ways: "I may not always be able to get through to your castle, but *you're* the real loser: you can't ever come out."

The Munchausen Syndrome

Karl Friedrich Hieronymus Frei-
herr von Munchausen, an eighteenth-century German baron,
fought against the Turks and then retired, at age forty, to his
estate. Thereafter, he spent his days as a writer and raconteur,
becoming a self-created legend by weaving incredible tales
about his experiences as a traveler, soldier, and sportsman. The
name Munchausen soon became synonymous with the fanciful
tall tale. Eventually, it was attached to a recognized psychiatric
condition, the *Munchausen Syndrome.*

Those afflicted with this personality disorder derive pleasure
from describing or simulating false symptoms of illness. The
typical sufferer prefers dramatic illnesses and seeks out exam-
inations, treatments, and hospitalization. Some are so skilled at
deception that they are able to con doctors into operating on
them; their bellies are often riddled with scars from all their
surgeries.

The Munchausen Syndrome should not be confused with hy-
pochondria—a preoccupation with bodily processes in which
any little sensation might lead to an irrational conviction that
one is sick. Victims of Munchausen are one step ahead: they
deliberately deceive their physicians. Although unaware of the
deeper personality problems their behavior represents, they are
typically intelligent and resourceful, sophisticated enough to
forge documents or simulate diseases by, say, adding blood to
urine or stool samples or heating up thermometers. They might
actually induce *real* symptoms, injecting themselves with bacte-
ria or feces, for example. According to the *Merck Manual,*
"individual patients can produce the clinical picture of myo-
cardial infarction, hematemesis or hemoptysis, acute abdomi-
nal conditions, or pyrexia of unknown origin. They can re-

produce symptoms of cerebral tumor or disseminated sclerosis with uncanny skill."

If you are not a physician or a therapist, you are unlikely to know a bona-fide victim of Munchausen Syndrome. That is, you might know one, but you are not likely to be aware of it; if the person can fool a doctor, he can no doubt trick friends and family into believing he's really sick. However, the term resonates so well with other forms of human deception that it deserves to be elevated to the status of a metaffect.

A metaffective form of Munchausen Syndrome was rampant in the 1960s, for example, although the cause was social and political, not psychiatric. Thanks to Vietnam, thousands of young men found ways to fabricate disorders that were known to earn draft deferments, often with the cooperation of sympathetic physicians. If universal conscription ever returns, another epidemic of Munchausen Syndrome is certain to follow, and you will have a name for it other than "draft dodger" or "malingerer."

If you are the parent of a resourceful son or daughter who prefers an occasional day in bed to attending school, you will have ample opportunity to use the phrase. The next time your child tries to con you into a day off by moaning and groaning and clutching his tummy and handing you a thermometer that he just dipped into hot water, you can knit your brow and sigh, "Oh, dear, you poor thing, we'd better get you to a psychiatrist. You've got a bad case of Munchausen Syndrome."

But why limit the term to its medical context? The original baron, after all, was a teller of tall tales that had nothing to do with illness. We can apply it to the fabrication of evidence to support all kinds of deceptions. Now you will know you are being munchausened when someone paints himself into pictures of exotic places that he's seen only in *National Geographic*, or when Granddad's war stories get more and more glorious with each subsequent telling, or when Auntie Mame reminisces about all the dashing young men who once pursued her lily-white hand.

The imaginative employee with forged letters to back up the histrionic story behind every lateness or absence can be accused of munchausening. The Don Juan whose tales of sexual exploits are accompanied by questionable names, places, photographs, and even an occasional trophylike pair of panties might be suffering from a variation of Munchausen Syndrome. So is the sympathy-seeker who invents all manner of domestic and romantic dramas in order to win your attention. If you search the box scores in vain for the name of an old codger who rhapsodizes about pitching against the 1927 Yankees, try looking under Munchausen instead. And when your husband comes home from a fishing trip and regales everyone he sees with stories about the one that got away, you can say, "Don't mind him. He developed a bad case of Munchausen Syndrome while he was away."

Admittedly, Munchausen tendencies can also be used to excellent advantage. Once I met a young cab driver who confided in me his trick for preventing boredom on the job. He would tell every passenger who struck up a conversation a different story about himself. He would gear his stories to the passenger: for young women he was an aspiring novelist; for older women, he was working his way through medical school and putting food on the table for his children; for men he might be doing undercover work, moonlighting to earn money for a trip around the world or supporting his training for the next Olympics. His Munchausen expertise not only made for more scintillating conversations but earned him excellent tips. (Come to think of it, he may have munchausened me.)

Some other uses of the term:

"If the Wilsons start going on about their vacation, let's

liven things up with a Munchausen version of our trip to Borneo."

"Maybe we shouldn't push Johnny into medical school, dear. Anyone with a Munchausen Syndrome like his should make movies or write novels. Or maybe go into advertising."

The temptation, of course, is to use the metaffect to deflate self-aggrandizing tellers of tall tales. But bear in mind one caveat: don't become a spoiled sport. Often enough, the Baron Munchausens are harmless, and they have wonderful entertainment value. There's a bit of the Munchausen Syndrome in each of us, and it makes the world a much more interesting place.

The Munich Syndrome

In the summer of 1938, Adolph Hitler demanded self-determination for ethnic Germans living in the Sudetenland region of Czechoslovakia. When the demand was rejected, riots broke out in the area and martial law was proclaimed by Czech authorities. Hitler, who coveted Sudetenland's rich mineral and industrial resources, amassed seven divisions on the border and announced that he would invade if the Czechs did not surrender the territory. War seemed inevitable; France was bound by treaty to fight for Czechoslovakia, and Britain would be compelled to aid the French.

On September 27, British Prime Minister Neville Chamberlain traveled to Munich to meet with Hitler, along with representatives from France and Italy. The English and French, loath to send their young men off to fight in a distant nation just two decades after the devastation of World War I, yielded to Hitler's demands. Sudetenland was handed over to Germany in return for a German promise to hold a plebiscite in the region and refrain from invading Czechoslovakia. Chamberlain considered this an honorable compromise. He believed it would satisfy Hitler's thirst for territory and halt Europe's slide into war. Upon his return to London, the Prime Minister triumphantly declared that he had brought back "peace in our time." Six months later, Nazi armies marched into Prague.

The *Munich Syndrome* quickly became synonymous with appeasement, defeatism, and cowardice in foreign affairs. Only two years later, Franklin D. Roosevelt invoked the incident to rebuke isolationists who did not want the United States to get involved in the war. And ever since, in reference to Korea, Berlin, Cuba, Vietnam, Afghanistan, and other places where international tension has erupted, hard-line hawks have cited the Munich Syndrome to make dovish liberals seem like yellow-bellied cowards playing into the hands of tyrants. In their view, giving in to the Communists—the successors to Nazis as global villains—would be to repeat Chamberlain's blunder and, through appeasement, let an earnest desire for peace lead us tripping down the primrose path to war. Even now, when the political Left compares U.S. involvement in Central America to Vietnam, the Right switches metaphors and compares it to Munich.

The Munich Syndrome assumes that it is categorically dangerous to think that your opponent shares your views of honor, trust, and peaceful coexistence. Those who conjure up Munich usually believe that peace can be attained only by demonstrating a willingness to fight, because conciliation will be interpreted as weakness and therefore an invitation to use force. Winston Churchill wrote that, given a choice between war and shame, Chamberlain chose shame and got war anyway.

As a metaffect, the Munich Syndrome need not be confined to international affairs. It is synonymous with giving in on a relatively small point in the hope of appeasing your opponent's appetite for greater gain. Labor strikes are often caused or prolonged by fear of the Munich Syndrome. To the public, both sides might appear stubborn for their refusal to compromise on minor issues, but behind the scenes are leaders who know that if they capitulate now, the other side will come to the table with even greater demands when the contract expires.

Suppose you are involved in a negotiation with an aggressive party and your legal advisers recommend giving in to a small demand for the sake of completing the deal. If you are looking ahead, your response might be, "If I yield that point, they'll think they can walk all over me, and next time they'll ask for even more. Hold firm. Let's not mortgage the future to the Munich Syndrome."

You can even use the principle in personal relationships. If your lover or spouse or roommate is on the demanding side, you might find yourself giving in on so many minor everyday issues that you establish a pattern of appeasement. Then, when a major conflict arises, the mold has been cast and you are expected to be just as agreeable as ever. Remember George Santayana's famous dictum, "Those who cannot remember the past are condemned to repeat it." If your own desires are being buried under a pile of concessions, you might want to invoke this historical precedent: "Who do you think I am, Neville Chamberlain? I refuse to be munched. I will not change the channel!"

Of course, many people fall back on the Munich Syndrome when the analogy is not really apt, playing on the emotions that the phrase elicits. Your competitor or client or lawyer or lover may not be as unprincipled as Hitler. There are times when Chamberlainlike strategies are safe, perhaps even advantageous. Therefore, you might find yourself arguing on behalf of actions that others view as cowardly appeasement: "I think we ought to concede that point. It's worth it to create a climate of goodwill for the future. I assure you, I am not Chamberlain and this is not the Munich Syndrome."

The NIMBY Reaction

Wouldn't it be great if someone invented a cheap, odor-free, nonpolluting, invisible way to get rid of garbage? Wouldn't it be nice if we could render harmless our toxic chemicals and radioactive wastes far from population centers? Unfortunately, no such technology exists. Neither does a laser gun that can zap waste products into thin air or a sanitation rocket launcher that can transport our garbage to another planet. What we're left with are waste-disposal methods that cause problems of their own: landfills that leach toxins into groundwater, incineration plants that pollute the air, garbage dumps that stink, and nuclear disposal sites that seep radioactivity. Even recycling centers have potential difficulties, not the least of which is traffic congestion. Out of this ecological predicament has come a new metaffect: the *NIMBY Reaction.*

NIMBY is not the last name of an ecologist; it is an acronym that stands for *Not in My Back Yard.* Not in My Back Yard, of course, is the place to which everyone would like to ship all pollutants, waste products, and other unwanted items. Someone else's backyard is also the preferred location for prisons, nuclear power plants, halfway houses for the mentally ill, shelters for the homeless, and drug rehabilitation centers.

Recently we were treated to a double NIMBY Reaction when residents of a Southern California community fought to keep a drug treatment facility out of their neighborhood. To show they meant business, they threatened to demonstrate outside the Bel-Air home of the project's chief sponsor, Nancy Reagan. The former First Lady's response was, essentially, "Demonstrations? Not in my backyard." And she withdrew her support for the project.

Although inadequate as a social policy, as a vocabulary item the NIMBY Reaction has great potential. Metaffectively, it signifies a self-absolving attitude with respect to social responsibility, an unwillingness to accept discomfort or risk for the common good. The next time someone knocks on your door with a petition to keep away from your neighborhood something that is socially useful but inconvenient, potentially hazardous, or simply undesirable, you'll know what to call it. If you're feeling particularly noble that day, you might say, "I refuse to sign any NIMBY petitions!"

The term is especially useful if you stretch the meaning of backyard. Suppose, for example, your family is in a financial crunch. Everyone recognizes the need for belt-tightening, but no one wants to give up his or her cherished expenditures. When your kids start whining, "I want to go to Disney World. You promised!" you know what to say: "I will not tolerate the NIMBY Reaction in this family. Everyone is going to have to sacrifice something."

The metaffect can be used in a similar way in business. When managers argue that their particular departments ought to be spared in a pending budget cut, or that someone else be made to break in the new trainees or start the day at eight A.M. to help alleviate traffic jams, you can simply respond, "Look, everyone's going to NIMBY this proposal, so let's save ourselves a lot of aggravation and just rotate the responsibility."

You can use the metaffect to spice up cocktail-party conver-

sations: "There's one simple reason why they'll never substantially reduce the budget deficit. Politicians get sanctimonious about responsible spending, but when push comes to shove they all take refuge in the NIMBY Reaction." Don't be surprised if someone adds, "You're right. And they also get attacks of NIMEY: Not in My Election Year."

The term can cover a multitude of ways that people deflect responsibility in favor of self-interest:

Call it the NIMBY Reaction when an office manager says, "I can't speak for other departments, but no one in mine is making unnecessary long-distance calls."

Suppose you are awakened in the middle of the night by the revving of car engines and the shrieks of electric guitars. If you complain to the teenagers next door, you might get a NIMBY Reaction like, "I swear, I was asleep by ten. It must have been those kids down the street."

Are your folks coming to visit for the holidays? Would you rather they stayed at your sister's house this year? You can head off trouble by saying, "Please don't NIMBY this again. Mom and Dad stay with us every year and you're the one with the big guest room."

Of course, you can always use the term with absolute literalness. Say your spouse asks you to host a barbecue for fifty or sixty business associates. Your answer: "NIMBY!"

The Nocebo Effect

The old "Laugh-In" show once had a vignette in which a doctor solemnly informs his aged patient of the results of an examination. He says, in effect, "Any sudden shock might kill you." There is a pause while the information registers. Then the patient keels over and dies.

Had they known the term then, the writers might have titled the sketch "The *Nocebo Effect.*"

The word *nocebo* might be unfamiliar, but most people know its opposite, *placebo*. A Latin word meaning "I shall please," placebo first appeared in medical literature in 1811, when it was defined as "an epithet given to any medicine adopted more to please than to benefit the patient." A contemporary medical dictionary defines it as "an inactive substance or preparation given to satisfy the patient's symbolic need for drug therapy and used in controlled studies to determine the efficacy of medicinal substances."

In recent years, placebos have come to be taken more seriously. While they may have no specific biological consequences, they can nevertheless enhance healing. Studies indicate that placebos have some measure of success in about one-third of all cases. Psychiatrist Jerome Frank attributes this to "the power of expectant faith." Evidently, merely *believing* that you have been given an effective remedy by someone in whom you have confidence can, in some mysterious way, actually help to alleviate symptoms. This is called the Placebo Effect, a recognized, although largely inexplicable, phenomenon (see also the Haelen Effect).

The flip side of the Placebo Effect is the Nocebo Effect, the *no-* possibly stemming from the Old English *ne* for "naughty," "nil," and "never." If the mind can be tricked, so to speak, into a set of beliefs that foster healing, it can surely be tricked in the opposite direction, shifting the body's capacity to heal into reverse. For the "Laugh-In" patient, the doctor's warning about shocks constituted precisely such a shock and the prophecy was fulfilled on the spot.

Dr. Deepak Chopra, author of *Quantum Healing,* is troubled by the possibility that doctors can create Nocebo Effects in the interest of accurate, honest reporting. He told an interviewer about a physician he had worked with years earlier. The man was a highly respected surgeon who worked long hours and smoked heavily. Troubled by his friend's persistent cough, Dr. Chopra one day suggested that he have an X ray. The surgeon replied, "No, there's no need; I've had this cough for years."

Dr. Chopra finally chided him into having an X ray. When the two physicians examined the results, they saw a lung lesion. The conclusion was obvious: the surgeon had cancer; according to statistics, he should be dead in three months. And, indeed, three months later he died.

Subsequently, Dr. Chopra looked at a set of his friend's X rays from three years earlier. He saw the same lung lesion. Evidently, it had escaped notice and the surgeon had never known about it. Says Chopra, "This was my first insight into what we are calling the nocebo. I said to myself, 'Did this fellow die of lung cancer, or of the diagnosis of lung cancer?'"

Lest anyone forget that what the mind giveth the mind can taketh away, we have this metaffect. I suspect it has a future in medicine. Imagine this scenario, which scientists say is not very far off. You are concerned that a particular disease, perhaps colon cancer, runs in your family. You submit a blood sample to a service, which freezes it in anticipation of a time when science is able to analyze your genes to see if you have in fact inherited a tendency toward the disease. The years pass, the technology advances, and you get a call: science can now determine precisely what your odds are of contracting colon cancer. Knowing about the Nocebo Effect, would you want to know?

The Nocebo Effect need not be confined to medicine; in essence, it refers to the mind's ability to conjure up grim or detrimental events—like the statistical death sentence given to Dr. Chopra's friend—through negative beliefs, assumptions, and discouraging information from others. How many books were not written, songs not composed, and canvases not painted because aspiring artists were noceboed into believing their chances of success were slim? How many children acquired a Jonah Complex (see page 128) because Miss Nocebo in the third grade convinced them they were stupid? How many worthwhile projects are canceled because naysayers create Nocebo Effects?

We nocebo ourselves all the time with sabotaging thoughts such as:

"Why even think about finding Mister Right? Half of all marriages end up in divorce."

"I'll never get into a decent law school. The odds are stacked against anyone with my background."

"The facts show that most people who quit smoking only start up again. Why bother to try?"

"Maybe I should give up this fantasy and get a regular job.

Statistics show that most small businesses fail in less than a year."

There's no escaping pessimistic prophecies, belligerent beliefs, and debilitating data, but you can prevent them from becoming Nocebo Effects. If someone casts a shadow on your life with statements like "It's hopeless. We'll never solve this problem on time," you can tell him, "Keep your nocebos to yourself. I prefer to believe it can be done."

The Nuisance Effect

"What we call progress," the British author Henry Havelock Ellis wrote in the early part of this century, "is the exchange of one nuisance for another nuisance." Economists might say that Ellis' cynical observation describes a phenomenon known as "technical external diseconomy," or the *Nuisance Effect*. In simple terms, it implies that apparently positive events often create unanticipated and undesirable repercussions, which have to be considered.

Here's how economists use the term. Due to the complexities of social and economic forces, decisions made for the good of an individual or an organization invariably reverberate in the larger society. Decisions frequently create nuisances—unexpected consequences that thwart the full attainment of societal objectives. For example, increased productivity can damage the environment; plant modernization can lead to heavy unemployment; the construction of an interstate highway might bankrupt a town on the old road. Such unwanted by-products of productive activities impose real costs and demand difficult decisions; hence the term Nuisance Effect.

Early in this century, the noted British economist A. C. Pigou advocated that society should bear the costs when economic conditions produce nuisances such as unemployment, poor health, or inadequate housing. Insofar as the unanticipated costs of economic events are allocated unevenly among different segments of society, Pigou contended, they ought to be considered a social problem, to be addressed by government.

Suppose the cost of producing railroad freight service is 3 cents per ton-mile, but the fires started by the trains' flying sparks cause crop damage amounting to half a cent per ton-mile. Pigou argued that the real cost of the steam locomotive is then 3.5 cents, not 3. Furthermore, he said, the responsibility for allocating the cost of that Nuisance Effect is a matter of social policy. Should the railroad pay the farmers for the crop damage? Should part of the cost be assessed to farmers who grow crops too close to railroad tracks? Should railroads be taxed or their operations restricted so as to prevent further damage? Or would such restraints impose even greater social costs than the damage to the crops? Indeed, at 3.5 cents per ton-mile, are steam locomotives worth using at all? To Pigou, questions like these are properly addressed by government.

Although "nuisance" might seem too tame a word for tragedies like air pollution and unemployment, the term Nuisance Effect can serve as a useful shorthand. Perhaps we'll soon see headlines such as "NEW FACTORY BOOSTS LOCAL ECONOMY, BUT CITIZENS CONCERNED ABOUT NUISANCE EFFECTS" or, perhaps, "CHINA DISCOVERS ECONOMIC EXPANSION CREATES NUISANCE EFFECTS."

But why confine the metaffect to macroeconomics? Life is filled with unforeseen nuisances whose costs have to be accounted for. Here are some examples.

"I wish someone had warned me about the Nuisance Effects of being a landlord. I might have sold these damn buildings and invested in art."

"Okay, I have no problem with your taking 75 percent of the profits, but one more thing before I sign the deal: who takes the responsibility for any Nuisance Effects that pop up down the road?"

"Paying for the mountain house was no problem, it was the Nuisance Effects—the four-wheel drive, the winter clothes, the fuel, someone to mind the place when we're not there . . . it all adds up."

Naturally, the costs of Nuisance Effects are not limited to money:

"I'm warning you, T.J., this guy's like one big Nuisance Effect. He gets the job done, no question about it, but there are always repercussions. He may be more trouble than he's worth."

"On the whole, I'm glad I got married. I just wish I'd calculated the psychological cost of the Nuisance Effects: the hair in the bathtub, the Monday-night football, the ex-wife, the lack of closet space. . . ."

Ockham's Razor

Did you ever know someone whose way of explaining things invariably turned out to be as complex and convoluted as a spy novel? Or someone whose theories seem logical but hinge on a bunch of assumptions whose veracity is questionable? For people like that, *Ockham's*

Razor is a worthwhile metaffect, although it was originally intended as a guidepost for scientists.

The term was named for William of Ockham, a fourteenth-century Franciscan philosopher and political theorist from the village of Ockham, in the county of Surrey, near London. In 1324, having spent more than a decade teaching at Oxford and writing outspoken political treatises, William was summoned to Avignon by Pope John XXII to answer charges of heresy. He waited for a verdict for fourteen years. Then, when he sided against the Pope on the question of evangelical poverty, things heated up and William fled to Bavaria. The Pope retaliated by excommunicating him, prompting twenty years of antipapal polemics from the exiled William's pen. He died in Munich in 1349, presumably of the Black Death.

William's name is remembered half a millennium later not because of his politics but because his "principle of parsimony," later known as Ockham's Razor, became a canon of faith in modern science.

As a guiding principle, Ockham's Razor is as economical as a Japanese car. Its axioms—such as "What can be done with fewer assumptions is done in vain with more" and "Entities are not to be multiplied without necessity"—boil down to this: the best theory is the simplest one. That is, one should eschew explanations that require a lot of assumptions and less-than-plausible hypotheses. The "entities" William referred to were demons, spirits, and other unprovable notions that in his day were frequently invoked to explain the inexplicable. William's philosophy reflects the conviction, now universally accepted, that nature works in an economical, elegant, and esthetically simple way, and therefore our explanations ought to reflect those same qualities.

In the sixteenth century, the principle of parsimony guided Copernicus to favor the heliocentric (sun-centered) theory of the solar system over the more popular geocentric (earth-centered) theory. Both hypotheses were capable of explaining the available data, but to Copernicus the orderly, symmetrical planetary orbits of the heliocentric model were more appealing, intellectually and esthetically. Scientists ever since have been guided by the same criteria; they are trained to prefer explanations that fit the facts but require the fewest hypotheses.

Ockham's Razor can be used as a guidepost for sorting out the intricacies of life. In search of understanding, we often confuse ourselves further with overly complicated deductions, piling inference upon hypothesis upon assumption. By remembering the principle, you can remind yourself to look for a simple explanation that fits the facts: "This is getting way too complicated. Let's use Ockham's Razor and cut through the crap."

Ockham can also be used to reverse the direction of anyone who expounds overly complicated theories and unsupportable hypotheses when a simple, factual explanation might do nicely. It provides you with a clever retort for someone who talks like this: "If you ask me, Bob had a subconscious need for the relationship to fail, and that played right into Sally's self-destructive tendencies, which are rooted in the low self-esteem she developed when her father abandoned her. Besides, she's an Aquarius, you know, so she's always a step ahead of the rest of us, but everyone acts like she's off the wall, so she never gets positive reinforcement for who she really is. So Bob, who's five foot five and has this need to make himself feel big by cutting off other people's heads, would criticize her a lot, and she'd get defensive, which probably reminded Bob of his mother, so he'd regress to this infantile state and . . ."

"Stop! Ockham the thing, willya? They were incompatible. Period."

If you find parsimony appealing, you will also like this corollary to Ockham's Razor: the principle of the least astonishing conclusion. According to geologist John W. Harrington in *The Dance of the Continents,* "scientists attempt to define their facts in absolute terms and recognize least astonishing solutions against a background of shared technical . . . experience." This gives you twin metaffects to use in the battle against muddled, labyrinthine reasoning: "I'm not naive, I just believe in the principle of least astonishing conclusions. And I'm in good company, too. Scientists have been thinking that way since William of Ockham honed his razor five hundred years ago."

Ah, but the razor is double edged: you can overdose on parsimony. In human affairs, sometimes the simple proposition is merely simplistic, and the one that fits the facts only appears to do so because you don't know enough of the facts. The least astonishing explanation may seem plausible only because you've made dubious assumptions or accepted bogus information as truth. What lurks beneath the surface of human intrigue is not always elegant or simple; often the truth *is* like a spy novel, and the best path to it meanders through the most astonishing intellectual terrain. Thus, at times, you might find yourself on the other side of the principle: "Let's not go crazy with Ockham's Razor, or we'll slice our intellects to ribbons. This might be more complicated than we think."

The Omnipotence Syndrome

In his book *The Uses of Disorder,* sociologist Richard Sennett decries the tendency of many urban planners to overplan, as if cities were machines whose parts can be ordained to mesh in a predictable way. The idea that the unpredictable, the sporadic, and the random can and should be eliminated, Sennett says, is a "godlike presumption about other people's lives," rooted in the urge "to be all powerful, to control the meaning of experience before encounter."

Harvard theologian Harvey Cox coined a term for what Sennett describes: the *Omnipotence Syndrome.* He extends the diagnosis beyond urban planners to "well-intentioned deans, doctors, ministers, social workers and business executives," and indeed to anyone who tries to control our complex, unpredictable world. To Cox, the compulsion to keep human conditions under control is a secular version of the biblical idea of sin. "We reach for the apple of omnipotence," he writes, meaning that we behave like Adam—with the temerity to try to be godlike. In Cox's view, those with a megalomaniacal need for control are doomed to defeat because rigid predictability runs contrary to the natural, spontaneous impulses of life.

We all know someone who plans compulsively. We call such a person a nitpicker, an anal retentive, or, if we are German, a *korinthenkacker* (literally, one who defecates raisins; colloquially, someone overly concerned with trivial details, according to Howard Rheingold, author of *They Have a Word For It*). Their businesses, their homes, even their vacations are charted to the second. When the unexpected enters their lives, as it inevitably does, they treat it like an invasion rather than an opportunity to learn or grow or profit materially.

The kind of people who earn the sobriquet "control freak," such as spouses who ride herd on their mates and have to have everything done their way, suffer from the Omnipotence Syndrome. Perhaps this metaffect will help those who live with omnipotents to get through to them by saying, "Loosen up, will you? We're not ants, we're humans. Go with the flow, or your Omnipotence Syndrome will suffocate all of us."

Other omnipotents include bosses who can't stop poking their noses into every corner of their subordinates' work. Driven by a need to feel important, they get furious if they don't hear from each employee every day. They spew forth a constant flow of memos and expect them answered posthaste. Able to delegate only the most mundane responsibilities, they take over the instant a problem arises and dictate what everyone will do to solve it. While they may succeed out of sheer tenacity and drive, they often fall short of their expectations, because their subordinates lack the autonomy to contribute their best. At their next job interviews, disgruntled employees can say, "I quit for health reasons: my boss had a bad case of the Omnipotence Syndrome."

The disease often strikes with no forewarning as soon as one becomes a parent; men and women with no previous symptoms suddenly start acting like Greek gods and goddesses, intervening in every aspect of their children's lives. Some parental illnesses have remarkable durability. In it for the long haul, afflicted parents select their child's college, curriculum, fraternity or sorority, extracurricular activities, and whole career plan. In extreme cases, this extends to exercising veto power over boyfriends and girlfriends and, eventually, governing *in absentia* the way their grandchildren are raised. Perhaps the next big support group will be Adult Children of Omnipotents.

Dealing with carriers of the Omnipotence Syndrome is one thing; purging it from your own personality is another. This requires a level of self-awareness that control freaks seldom attain, so busy are they molding their environments into predictable spheres of influence. Perhaps if this metaffect catches on, some will be spared. Meanwhile, one should be on the lookout for warning signs: extreme intolerance of ambiguity; fear and trembling in the face of uncertainty; temper tantrums when things don't go one's way; excessively rigid routines; inability to grant autonomy to others; and getting flustered by life's detours, cancellations, accidents, and other caprices.

Omnipotence is a tough habit to break. You just might find yourself saying, "Damn, I thought I had that Omnipotence Syndrome licked, but I can't bring myself to let anyone else run those meetings."

The Pareto Principle

Have you ever had the feeling that most of what you accomplish is achieved through only a small portion of the things you do to reach your goals? If so, you should appreciate the *Pareto Principle*.

An economist and sociologist in the late nineteenth and early twentieth centuries, Vilfredo Pareto became famous for applying mathematics to economic theory and for his analysis of social class structures. At one point, Pareto calculated that 80 percent of Italy's income was being earned by 20 percent of the population. This led to the formulation of the Pareto Principle, or the 80/20 Law. It boils down to this: 20 percent of the effort produces 80 percent of the results.

Pareto's proportion suggests that the constellation of elements required to fulfill a goal are organized in a hierarchy of importance; a small percentage are so critical that they are directly responsible for the bulk of the results. The trick, of course, is to know which activities constitute that highly productive 20 percent. Theoretically, if you could devote your time exclusively to the critical factors, you would achieve 80 percent of your goals. On the other hand, if you miscalculate and focus on the least productive elements, you will end up spending four times as much time and energy to reach only 20 percent of your goals.

In management circles, a story is told about Charles Schwab, then president of Bethlehem Steel. About fifty years ago, Schwab asked a famous management consultant named Ivy Lee to help him make more productive use of his time. Lee gave Schwab these instructions: before leaving the office, list the next day's most important tasks in order of significance; the next morning, begin the day by working on the most important task and stay with it until it is completed; then move on to the second task and work on it until it is finished, and so on. If a single task happens to take all day, Lee advised, stick with it as long as it remains the most important of the lot.

(Lee suggested a unique way to determine his consultation fee: after trying his method, Schwab would pay whatever he thought the advice was worth. A few weeks later, Schwab gave the consultant a check for $25,000, a hefty sum back then. He later said that it was the single most important investment that Bethlehem Steel made that year.)

Whether you adhere to Ivy Lee's method or find some other way to organize your time, the Pareto Principle might be a useful guidepost for separating critical tasks from the noncritical. A number of management experts believe the 80/20 principle is an accurate rule of thumb. Says time-management consultant Merill Douglass, "You can bet your life—or your business—on the Pareto Principle."

The next time you think that your colleagues are spending too much time on minor activities and not enough on crucial ones, you can invoke one of history's leading economists in urging them to rearrange priorities: "I strongly suggest that from now on we run this place according to the Pareto Principle. Let's make a list of everything we have to do and divide it into two columns: critical and noncritical. We need to find the vital 20 percent."

The Pareto Principle has been applied successfully in a number of areas. In some cases, 80 percent of revenues come from 20 percent of the customers, or from 20 percent of the total number of products for sale. Eighty percent of the best work in your company may be done by 20 percent of your workers. Perhaps 20 percent of your advertising generates 80 percent of your response, or 20 percent of your investments yield 80 percent of your interest income. One of every five phone calls might be four times as productive as the other four calls combined, and forty-eight minutes of every hour spent in meetings might be relatively ineffectual compared to the twelve minutes of excellent communication. Knowing the Pareto Principle might lead you to such fruitful observations.

Let's take the concept outside the realm of business. Do you derive four times as much pleasure from what you do with one-fifth of your leisure time, while the other four-fifths delivers paltry enjoyment? Do one-fifth of the sitcoms you watch trigger four times as many laughs as all the others combined? Perhaps the principle applies to the mind: does one of every five thoughts generate 80 percent of your imaginative ideas? If you are a student, does one of your classes provide four times the intellectual excitement as the other four? Do you derive four-fifths of your useful information from 20 percent of what you read?

What about relationships? Do one-fifth of your acquaintances command 80 percent of your loyalty? Are four out of five conversations a waste of time, while the other 20 percent are four times as stimulating? Does 80 percent of the pleasure you get from your love affair come from a certain 20 percent of the time you spend together? I can hear the bedroom repartee now:

"You come over for five hours, and the only time you seem really interested in me is the one hour we spend in bed."

"There's nothing wrong with that, darling. It's perfectly normal. They call it the Pareto Principle."

Pauli's Exclusion Principle

In 1925, when he enunciated this concept, Wolfgang Pauli was a twenty-five-year-old prodigy who looked like the young Al Capone. The Austrian physicist, who would later win a Nobel Prize for postulating the existence of the neutrino twenty-six years before it was actually observed, was called the archetypal theoretical physicist by Stephen Hawking, the author of *A Brief History of Time*. "It was said of him," Hawking writes, "that even his presence in the same town would make experiments go wrong!"

Pauli's Exclusion Principle, which became a cornerstone of modern physics, states that no two electrons in an atom may be in the same quantum, or energy, state. Each electron is unique; no two particles can have the same spin or occupy the same orbit. "This place ain't big enough for both of us," says one electron to another, according to Pauli. If not for the Exclusion Principle, atoms would not be discrete entities, and matter would constantly fall apart.

Metaffectively, the concept is quite useful. Many areas of human life operate under a kind of Exclusion Principle. For example, like electrons, humans shift from one energy state to another but can occupy only one at a time. You're either tired or fresh, weak or strong—not both. The same is true for our many moods, attitudes, and emotions. On those occasions when you feel ambivalent or mixed up, the Exclusion Principle might serve as a reminder that you can be in only one state of consciousness at a time. This can simplify matters tremendously, requiring that you settle on one mode of feeling, presumably the strongest or most useful one.

Suppose you feel confused about a relationship because your status is ill-defined. Maybe it's time to confront your lover: "We're at the Pauli point. I'm like an electron that can't exist in two states at once: either we're in a committed relationship or we're not. Which will it be?"

Or suppose, at work, you are caught in a familiar managerial dilemma: you're given responsibility but not enough authority to carry out an expeditious policy. You might cut through the confusion by telling your boss: "I need to apply the Exclusion Principle to my job description. Either give me complete authority or absolve me of responsibility for the outcome."

You might also invoke Pauli when too much is demanded of you, as in, "I'm sorry, sir, but my mind works according to the Exclusion Principle: if it pays attention to more than one thing at a time, it shifts into a lower energy state."

Pauli's Exclusion Principle is a fresher and more distinctive way of proclaiming the uniqueness of each individual than the redundant evocation of snowflakes. Like electrons, no two people, however similar, can have exactly the same orientation. If your boss fails to appreciate your singular value, you might give him a physics lesson: "I don't care to be lumped into some category with everyone else. According to the Exclusion Principle, no one else can occupy my particular niche but me. I spin in my own orbit."

Even our perception operates according to an Exclusion Principle of sorts; we shift from one point of view to another, never occupying more than one at a time. The way we evaluate people and events changes as our state of awareness changes. Consider your attitude toward those around you when you are tired or depressed, as compared to when you are well-rested and happy. Similarly, no two people can possibly see things in exactly the same way; we each put our own spin and orientation on things. When your viewpoint is irreconcilable with another's, it may be useful to say, "Look, we'll never see eye to eye on this, so let's chalk it up to the Exclusion Principle and agree to disagree."

Perhaps our social systems mimic the atomic building blocks of which we are made. Consider how, in rigid hierarchies and class systems, whole categories of people are relegated to the outer orbits of social or economic status, far from the nucleus, where the power is. A privileged elitist might indeed consider Pauli's Principle proof that exclusion is the natural way to organize things. (In fact, statutes prohibiting certain groups of people from voting were once known as "exclusion laws.")

Those of us with more egalitarian outlooks need to point out one thing: Pauli's Principle holds that only one particle can occupy a given position at a time, but it does not specify which particle. Matter is in a constant state of flux. Just as the electrons in atoms are always changing, new ones replacing the old like the cells on our skin, there is a parallel social mobility in human affairs. Subject to the vagaries of time, the whims of the masses, the vicissitudes of fame, those now close to the nucleus of power can one day be booted to the outer orbits. Call it the Bob Dylan Corollary to the Exclusion Principle: "The first one now will later be last, for the times they are a'changing."

The Pike Syndrome

The pike is a long, lean fish with a dorsal fin and a mouth filled with sharp, curved teeth. Its meat is quite delicious, but the fish is prized by game fishermen more for sport than taste; pikes are tenacious fighters. In their own undersea world, they are ferocious predators whose principal prey are smaller fish. Indeed, it was their predation habits that led to the discovery of the *Pike Syndrome*.

As explained by management consultant Karl Albrecht in his book *Brainpower*, "ordinarily a pike will quickly devour any minnow it finds swimming in its neighborhood. When researchers lower a bell jar into the pike's aquarium and put minnows into it, the pike will lunge at them many times, bumping its face painfully on the glass barrier. After many tries, it gives up and ignores them. When the researchers remove the bell jar so the minnows can swim around freely, the pike never tries to eat them. The minnows can swim all around the pike and right past its nose, but it will not attack. It has become fully fixated in its behavior, unable to adapt to a new reality. It may even eventually starve surrounded by an abundant food supply."

Albrecht views the Pike Syndrome as a metaphor for rigid, conditioned thinking. The fixated pike is unable to realize that what he learned no longer makes sense because conditions have changed. Destructive at worst, self-limiting at best, the condition is a form of what anthropologist Ashley Montagu called "psychosclerosis," a kind of hardening of the mental arteries that inhibits the flow of ideas and narrows life's possibilities.

The term can be applied as a metaffect to any self-defeating mental fixation. Like a pike who denies itself a good meal in order to avoid banging its head against a glass wall that's no longer there, we often miss out on opportunities because we've locked ourselves into rigid patterns of thought. To a certain degree, we are all susceptible to the kind of conditioning that creates the Pike Syndrome. Perhaps knowing the term will help you spot it in yourself as well as others.

Victims of the Pike Syndrome are fixated; despite an abundance of new evidence, they haven't learned that circumstances change and new possibilities abound. The next time you spot a pike, hook it and reel it in with your new metaffect:

"Don't pike out of giving the speech. So what if you forgot your lines in the high school play. You're thirty years old now, and you're very articulate."

"Look, I'm sorry if your first marriage was a disaster, but I'm tired of being strung along. I want a man, not a pike."

"You probably don't need the cane now. It was useful when

you had a broken foot, but the only thing wrong with you now is the Pike Syndrome."

"Dad, you're hooked by the Pike Syndrome. Take that money out from under the mattress. Bank deposits have been insured since the Great Depression."

"But this is the best restaurant on Fisherman's Wharf. I assure you, their chef does a better job with salmon than your mother did."

The Pike Syndrome is tough to shake; the afflicted have bumped their heads against the glass so many times that they can't see the lovely minnows swimming all around them. If some past experience has closed your mind to life's possibilities, hope that someone baits you with this metaffect.

The Principles of Least Time and Least Action

Pierre de Fermat was a seventeenth-century French magistrate who achieved posterity not for anything associated with the legal profession, but for his avocation, mathematics. His name is linked to four discoveries: Fermat's Law, a principle in optics; Fermat's Spiral; Fermat's Last Theorem (which mathematicians accept as true but have never been able to prove); and *Fermat's Principle of Least Time.*

This last principle states that light traveling from one point to another always takes the path that uses the least amount of time. Evidently, a beam of light values its time as much as any executive with an eye on the bottom line; it will never bend or curve or loop around or take the scenic route if a more expedient path is available. Fermat had very little evidence to back up his theory; his conviction was based on the belief that God designed nature's workings and God must be a supremely efficient architect. Scientists have since compiled other evidence.

Here we have a timely metaffect for our hypercharged era. The next time the accounting department asks why you take the Concorde instead of an ordinary jet or why you fly from New York to Washington instead of taking Amtrak; the next time your spouse wants to meander through the countryside on the way to the family reunion or do some window shopping on the way to a business luncheon; the next time your suppliers ask for an extension on a deadline, you'll know what to say: "I follow Fermat's Principle of Least Time. If it's good enough for a beam of light, it's good enough for me. God [or Nature, if you prefer] built us to be efficient."

(Of course, the other party might point out that nature, or God, might not care for your wasting money or neglecting to stop and smell the flowers; Fermat is of no help there.)

Speed is only one aspect of time; another is duration. Metaffectively, the Principle of Least Time can also be applied to the number of hours or days one spends on a task. You can use the metaffect when quickness is a virtue. Sometimes the first idea is the most fertile one, the first impulsive effort the most efficient. Some projects get stale if they drag on; polish them too much and they acquire an overworked, glitzy sheen. And, of course, some tasks just have to be completed so you can get on to more important things. If your employees, family, or friends need some prodding, try this: "Let's set our clocks to Fermat time—the least time possible to get this done."

You can spice up Fermat with a complementary metaffect, the *Principle of Least Action*, the product of another Frenchman, Pierre-Louis Moreau de Maupertius. Building on Fermat's Principle about a century later, Maupertius asserted that nature works so as to make any event require the least possible action.

He backed up his theory with physical examples, principally the movement of particles. But, like Fermat, his main inspiration was theological. As mathematician Morris Kline describes it, "the laws of the behavior of matter had to possess the perfection worthy of God's creation and the least action principle seemed to satisfy the criterion because it showed that nature was economical. Maupertius proclaimed his principle to be a universal law of nature and the first scientific proof of the existence and wisdom of God."

In time (the *least* time, perhaps), the religious justification of scientific principles was abandoned by the heirs of Fermat and Maupertius. But nature's fundamental efficiency was confirmed and expanded. In fact, some scientists contend that virtually every physical law can be viewed as a least action principle, since nature always prefers effortless economy.

When might least action be appropriate? When a dignified silence speaks more eloquently than angry words. When the stock market plunges and everyone panics but you stay put, neither buying nor selling. When you've done such effective preliminary work that an operation can run itself. When you've trained your subordinates so thoroughly that you can safely delegate and keep your mind on the big picture. When your child asks for help but you know he'll learn more if he muddles through by himself. When all around you are losing their heads and you've achieved the Meissner Effect (see page 136). When you need to think.

Bear in mind that when humans take the path of least action, it is sometimes difficult to determine whether they are being efficient, as nature intended, or just plain lazy. People in occupations that require a lot of cogitation are especially vulnerable to the charge of indolence. Mark Twain once used this defense: "Just because I'm not writing doesn't mean I'm not writing."

Since the American work ethic implies a principle of *most*

action, you might need a way to explain yourself when you choose the opposite route. If you are convinced that nose-to-the-grindstone stress, strain, and struggle will not produce the most effective results, you might say, "I think in this case doing less can accomplish more. I'm not lazy, I'm simply following a natural law: the Principle of Least Action."

Least Time, Least Action. If you need support for these metaffects, you might invoke the ancient Chinese philosopher Lao Tse, who said that the wise man "does nothing, yet he leaves nothing undone."

❦

The Prisoner's Dilemma

Imagine that you and a partner have committed an armed robbery and in the process an innocent person was killed. You are both apprehended and placed in separate cells with no way to communicate. If prosecuted, you will almost certainly be convicted of robbery. However, there is not enough evidence to make a murder charge stand up—unless one of you confesses. The authorities come to your cell and offer a deal: you, and only you, will be let off scot-free, with both charges against you dropped, if you confess to murder . . . and your partner does *not* confess. If you *both* confess, you will both be charged with murder but given a reduced sentence. If neither of you confesses, the robbery charge will stand and you will surely be convicted.

What would you do?

The problem, of course, is that you have no way of knowing whether your partner has been offered the same deal, and if he has, what his decision will be. The best possible scenario for you is to confess while your partner does not. The worst is for you *not* to confess while he tells all. (If that happens, he walks away free and you stand trial for both the murder and the robbery.) In between are these possibilities: neither of you confesses and you both end up with robbery convictions, or both of you confess and you are charged with robbery plus a reduced murder rap.

The only possible way to stay out of jail is to confess . . . but what if your partner does the same? Then you are both worse off than you would have been if you had kept your mouths shut. Short of telepathic communication between jail cells, nothing can diminish the uncertainty and agony of the *Prisoner's Dilemma*.

The Prisoner's Dilemma is actually a problem devised by game theorists to illustrate the complexity of political choices. Its formal structure has been applied to the arms race, income policies, environmental issues, and other areas of social life where personal decisions have consequences beyond the individual. According to one expert, the Prisoner's Dilemma "captures a kind of insight about the contrary effects of individually rational decisions."

The dilemma of the two prisoners is paralleled in real-life situations. Consider the true story told by Bulgarian writer Georgi Markov of a resistance fighter during World War II, who was offered two choices when he was captured. First, he could inform on his comrades, in which case his captors would sentence him to death but arrange for his secret escape. Then, once he was freed, another resistance fighter would be killed and false papers planted on him to indicate that he, not our hero, betrayed his allies. By taking the second option, the prisoner could protect the identities and locations of his comrades. However, he would be executed, and as soon as someone else informed on the resistance (as surely someone would), forged papers would prove that our hero was the real betrayer, and his name would live in infamy. Faced with this dilemma, the prisoner found a third alternative: he went mad.

As a metaffect, the Prisoner's Dilemma can be used when one is faced with any perplexing decision whose impact extends beyond oneself. Suppose you've told two white lies to protect two people and they turn out to contradict each other. Which lie will you expose, at which person's expense? Suppose you gave a friend a tip on a stock only to discover something new that dictates reversing your recommendation, but sharing the new information would constitute a violation of insider trading rules. Do you inform your friend and put yourself in jeopardy?

Here is a situation based on a true story. You own a factory and you learn about a new chemical process by which you can save a great deal of money, thus improving your profit margin. Unfortunately, the process will pollute a nearby river and, possibly, the local drinking water—although you probably won't get caught, because the chemicals are very hard to trace. So far, it sounds like you have an easy choice: you can't, in good conscience, pollute the environment to make a few more bucks.

Now add this to the equation: your business is losing money and you are on the verge of laying off workers, thus endangering the welfare of dozens of families. The new chemical process might save those jobs. On top of that, you have good reason to believe that your successful competitor upstream is also aware of the new process and just might decide to use it, in which case not only will your business slip into further trouble, but the river will be polluted anyway. You need help: "Fellow board members, we are faced with a Prisoner's Dilemma."

Another example is from the battle zone of love. Suppose, in a moment of weakness, you go out on a date with George. But George has been seeing your friend Alice, who takes the liaison rather seriously. You have a great time and George wants to see you again, but you decide not to go any further with the relationship in deference to your friendship with Alice. However, while George is taking you home, you inadvertently discover that he is also having an affair with a second friend, Barbara.

You are torn: for Alice's sake, you feel you ought to tell the truth about George's shameless philandering. However, if you do, you not only come between Alice and Barbara, but your own indiscretion will be revealed. Then again, confessing might be preferable to having Alice find out through other means that you went out with George. You could consult a noted authority:

"Dear Abby, what am I to do? I have one of those pesky Prisoner's Dilemmas on my hands."

"Dear Prisoner: Unless you want to go mad, consult the Chappaquidick Theorem on page 53 of *The Babinski Reflex* by Philip Goldberg, and learn the lesson that history can teach."

The Pygmalion and Hawthorne Effects

In Ovid's *Metamorphoses*, Pygmalion, King of Cyprus, was a gifted sculptor and an unrepentant misogynist, "detesting the faults beyond measure which nature has given to women." He vowed never to marry, instead devoting his full energies to his sculpture. However, Pygmalion must have been repressing a deep-seated adoration of women, or at least their physical attributes, because he labored obsessively to create a statue of the perfect female form, refining and reworking it until it was more exquisite than any woman or statue had ever been.

By the time he was finished, Pygmalion had fallen deeply

and passionately in love with his creation. Since being in love with a hunk of stone, however lovely and lifelike, is the ultimate in unrequited love, he flirted with madness. He kissed his statue, whom he'd named Galatea, caressed her unresponsive face, dressed her, and laid gifts at her perfect feet. Utterly forlorn, Pygmalion beseeched Venus, the goddess of love, to send him a maiden the equal of his incomparable statue. Touched by this singular supplicant, Venus went one step better: she turned Galatea into a living woman and even attended her wedding to Pygmalion.

Ovid's tale has been retold and adapted many times, of course, in Marston's *Metamorphosis of Pygmalion's Image;* Morris' *The Earthly Paradise;* W. S. Gilbert's *Pygmalion and Galatea,* a nineteenth-century comedy; and, most recognizably, in George Bernard Shaw's *Pygmalion,* whose Henry Higgins and Eliza Doolittle would later sing their tale in *My Fair Lady.* But it is a scientist's use of the myth that gave rise to the term *Pygmalion Effect.*

In the 1960s, Harvard psychologist Robert Rosenthal conducted an experiment in which he randomly divided grade-school students into two groups, carefully matched by age, sex, ethnic background, and IQ scores. Rosenthal told the students' teachers before the start of the school year that one group consisted of fast learners while the others were merely average. A year later, when he compared the achievement of the two groups, Rosenthal found that the performance of the "fast learners" far surpassed that of the "average" students. The marked difference in academic success was attributed principally, if not exclusively, to the expectations of the teachers. They treated one group as if it were outstanding and it became so, just as Pygmalion treated his statue as if it were real and it became so.

The phenomenon, which was subsequently confirmed by a number of experiments, was named by Rosenthal, who recounted his research in a 1968 book, *Pygmalion in the Classroom: Teacher Expectation and Pupil's Intellectual Development.* It has also been called the Rosenthal Effect and the Experimenter Effect. The metaffect embodies the enormous impact that beliefs, biases, and expectations have on the outcome of events. It suggests that people tend to live up to what is expected of them, even if they are not aware of those expectations. More specifically, it indicates that we can change other people by virtue of our own beliefs, even if those beliefs are erroneous.

Armed with Rosenthal's discovery, if you suspect that the teachers in your child's school are having an anti-Pygmalion impact on the students, you can tell your spouse, "Honey, the people running Linda's school have mediocre expectations for their students. I want her to transfer to a place that can have a Pygmalion Effect on her future."

Suppose you've hired a new coach in hopes of reversing your team's sorry record. If your personal ethics can tolerate a little white lie, why not tell the coach that his new players have been hand-picked by crack recruiters for their superior athletic potential? By raising the coach's expectations—and, no doubt, his zeal for the job—you might set off a chain reaction that leads to a Pygmalion story like that of the 1969 Mets.

The same can be done in business, of course. If you are interviewing candidates to take over a department, select the one whose standards are unusually high. Tell your partners, "Sure, her expectations are off the wall, but maybe she can pull off a Pygmalion Effect and turn those lumps of clay into real workers."

In business circles, another, closely related metaffect is well known: the *Hawthorne Effect.* In the late 1920s, industrial psychologists measuring the impact of various working conditions on productivity inadvertently made a discovery that would have a major impact on management practices.

At a plant in Hawthorne, Illinois, the researchers selected

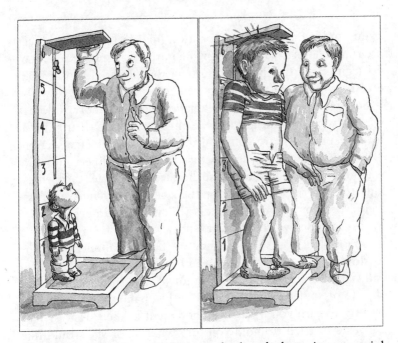

several assembly-line workers and placed them in a special room where their work environment could be systematically altered. The purpose was to see how different conditions affected productivity. Certain changes (including dimmer lighting and shorter workdays) were expected to lower productivity, while others (such as a pay raise, better temperature, and improved lighting) were expected to increase the workers' output. What happened astonished the scientists: productivity went up under *every* new condition, even those expected to have the reverse effect. Interviews with the subjects revealed that they felt special because they had been selected to participate in something different; it seemed that the company cared about them and their working conditions. The resulting *esprit de corps* made possible their record-breaking productivity.

This serendipitous discovery—workers who are made to feel special will produce more—was named after the location of the plant, and it had a direct impact on how factories and offices are run. In effect, without knowing it, the Hawthorne researchers legitimized the Pygmalion Effect four decades before Robert Rosenthal's educational experiment.

Some people are natural Pygmalions, or Hawthornes: lovers who know how to keep romance alive by making their beloved feel exceptional (have you read the Acknowledgments section, dear?); commanders who can turn mediocre soldiers into elite warriors by treating them as such; parents who get their eldest kids to take responsibility for their siblings by making them feel favored or improve an underachieving child's performance by turning homework into an event.

There is, of course, a flip side to the Pygmalion Effect: the world according to Galatea and Eliza Doolittle. Both of them had happy endings, but that is not always the case with the objects of someone's attempt to be Pygmalion. Did your parents try to turn you into the embodiment of their desires? Has a lover ever tried to mold you into what he or she would like you to be? Perhaps knowing the metaffect will help you recognize destructive Pygmalions before it's too late: "I can't see you any more, Fred. You're trying to make me into something I don't wish to be, and I won't be a victim of the Pygmalion Effect."

Finally, consider the impact the use of this metaffect can have on the Pygmalion figure himself. Many a would-be Pygmalion has ended up bemoaning the hubris that made him think he could sculpt another person like a chunk of marble. Dr. Frankenstein was a Pygmalion character. So are the parents who try to turn young mechanical geniuses into lawyers, and the dictators who run nations into the ground by forcing their minions to act against their natures. True, the original Pygmalion ended up with his heart's desire, and *My Fair Lady* has a happy ending, but along the way, Pygmalion was making love to a rock and Henry Higgins went through his share of personal upheavals. In some ways, the transformers were transformed more profoundly than Galatea and Eliza Doolittle.

Anyone who hopes to execute a Pygmalion Effect, therefore, should bear in mind this caveat: you can't change someone else without going through changes yourself.

The Salieri Phenomenon

Antonio Salieri was a conductor-composer of modest talent whose real gift was as a tutor rather than an artist. Among his students were such greats as Liszt, Schubert, and Beethoven. In his role as court conductor in Vienna in the late eighteenth and early nineteenth centuries, Salieri was the custodian of patronage for aspiring musicians and composers, a man who could open the door of opportunity or block it. By all accounts, he was generous to those whose talents were less than or equal to his own and whose values and behavior would not threaten the status quo.

Enter a young man who fit none of those criteria: Wolfgang Amadeus Mozart. Anyone who has seen the movie *Amadeus,* or the Peter Shaffer play on which it was based, knows that Mozart was a brash nonconformist whose transcendent genius drove Salieri mad with envy. Mozart also had a gift for vulgarity and frankness that offended the polite etiquette of the court, and his musical ideas not only challenged existing standards but threatened Salieri's own status. Salieri could hardly have kept Mozart's genius a secret, but he was able to prevent the upstart from receiving recognition and rewards commensurate with his accomplishments. The way he went about this prompted sociologist Judith Lorber to coin a new term: the *Salieri Phenomenon.*

Dr. Lorber, a professor at Brooklyn College and the Graduate Center of the City University of New York, summarizes the phenomenon as "undermining someone's career in the guise of doing a favor," or damning with faint praise. In her book *Women Physicians: Careers, Status and Power,* Lorber illustrates her point with a passage from Shaffer's play. The obsequious Salieri discusses Mozart with his patron, Emperor Joseph:

JOSEPH: We must find him a post.
SALIERI: There's nothing available, Majesty.
JOSEPH: There's Chamber Composer, now that Gluck is dead.
SALIERI: (Shocked) Mozart to follow Gluck?
JOSEPH: I won't have him say that I drove him away. You know what a tongue he has.
SALIERI: Then grant him Gluck's post, Majesty, but not his salary. That would be wrong.
JOSEPH: Gluck got two thousand florins a year. What should Mozart get?
SALIERI: Two hundred. Light payment, yes, but for light duties.
JOSEPH: Perfectly fair. I'm obliged to you, Court Composer.

Over time, Salieri pretended to champion the young composer while actually blocking his advancement by denigrating his worth and making sure his rewards were minimal. In subsequent scenes we see that Mozart was fooled into thinking Salieri was his benefactor.

According to Dr. Lorber, the Salieri Phenomenon lives today in the medical profession, where female physicians seldom achieve the same level of advancement as male colleagues of equal ability. In her twenty-year longitudinal study, Lorber found that by mid-career women doctors lagged behind men whose initial performance was of similar quality. The principal reason, she concluded, was that advancement is based largely on the sponsorship of established physicians, the bulk of whom are men. As in most subcultures, the inner circle favors those with whom they feel most comfortable—essentially, the colleagues who are most like themselves.

"In modern times," writes Lorber, "the Salieri phenomenon is used in recommendations for positions, promotions, and officerships in professional associations, in reviews and in citations of published work and work-in-progress, and in professional shoptalk that evaluates the competence of colleagues." Dr. Lorber points out that the phenomenon is found in other professions as well and affects other social groups whose members are not in the inner circle.

The Salieri Phenomenon can apply to all manner of sabotage. The metaffective lesson is to keep a watchful eye on those who praise you and offer their assistance; they might be subtle saboteurs. A few examples:

Say you're interested in buying a rental property. A friend tells you that his cousin is about to put a building on the market and is willing to sell at a terrific price. You call your broker. He sees the property and praises its virtues, but he also points out potential problems of which you were unaware. The bottom line, he says, is that the investment has merit but not as much as a second, more expensive property that he knows about. You take his advice and buy the second property. Then he buys the building you showed him. You've been salieried.

Your boss values your word-processing skills so highly that he grants you perks, gives you small periodic raises, and praises you to the skies. But you are never considered for promotion to a supervisory position. This irks you; you feel that with a little experience you can manage other people as well as anyone in the company. You realize your boss has sabotaged your advancement because he doesn't want to lose you. It's time to tell the employment agency, "I need a change. My boss is a nice guy, but I'm locked into a dead end because of the Salieri Phenomenon."

You meet a man you're very interested in. He just might be

Mister Right. You introduce him to your parents, and later gush, "Isn't he wonderful? You should see his paintings. When his style catches on, he'll be a famous artist."

Your mother says, "I'll bet he looks quite nice without that beard."

Your father says, "I hear your ex-boyfriend was made chief of surgery."

You put your foot down. "That's the last time I'll introduce you to anyone. You always try to salieri my relationships."

At times we might even play Salieri to our own Mozart. We sabotage ourselves in various ways, keeping ourselves from reaching our goals because of guilt, fear of success, or a subconscious sense of inadequacy. If you find yourself gratefully accepting a position lower than the one you deserve, or committing to a relationship that doesn't measure up to your ideals, it's time to tell youself, "Hey, Mozart! Don't salieri yourself again."

Say's Law

The French economist Jean Baptiste Say (1767–1832) is noted by historians for reorganizing and popularizing the theories of English economist Adam Smith and for developing both a theory of markets and the concept of the entrepreneur. He is also remembered for the principle that bears his name. Simply put, *Say's Law* says "supply creates its own demand."

According to Say, the act of production itself should generate enough income to purchase all the goods produced. Households supply resources to the business sector, namely, workers.

In return, the workers who produce goods are paid for their efforts, and that pay enables them to purchase the goods they help to produce. Say postulated that the process of production therefore ensures that the goods produced will be purchased. Unfortunately, when society became more industrial and economies grew to be more complex, Say's Law no longer held up universally.

Nevertheless, as a metaffect, the law has interesting possibilities in instances where a supply of something generates a demand for it or where abundance makes something more attractive than it might otherwise be. Proof of Say's Law is all around you. No one demanded Post-Its or Fax machines until someone with foresight supplied them. You didn't know you wanted an electric pencil sharpener, but now you're using one. You thought you didn't want dessert, but then the waiter wheeled in the pastry cart. You probably didn't know there was a demand for a book of metaffects, but here you are reading one.

One influence on the marketplace that Say never conceived of is sophisticated advertising. As we all know, a healthy supply of repetitive sounds and images creates a demand independent of the product itself. Once they hear about this metaffect, advertising executives will be saying, "I want to make that logo as ubiquitous as sunlight. We'll apply Say's Law until the public clamors for our product."

You can use Say's Law to your benefit too. Did you ever wish you had a clever rejoinder when your spouse criticized you for spending money on something no one needs? Now you can call on economic theory when you unpack those boxes of Christmas decorations you picked up on sale, or the third television you couldn't resist, or the little kitchen gadget the salesman said no home should be without, or that new set of dishware: "Why did I buy this? Because of Say's Law, that's why. Now that we have it, we're sure to use it."

The law can be used as a motivational tool as well. You might use it to get your kids to study: "I can't tell you exactly how studying history will be relevant in your future. But I can tell you this: there is a kind of Say's Law of the mind. The more knowledge you have, the more you'll find a way to use it."

The metaffect can also replace "Because it's there." Used by mountaineers to explain why they wanted to climb Mount Everest, the phrase has since been picked up by so many others with outlandish dreams that it's probably being used just because it's there. Now you can say it differently: "Why do I want to water ski across Lake Michigan? To honor Say's Law. The presence of the lake demands that it be conquered."

Watch out, though, because Say's Law has its down side too. Hence, you might find a use for a metaffective backlash, such as:

"I don't care what Say's Law says. We don't have to watch television just because we have four sets."

"There is too much use of the Xerox machine in this office. I'm going to reverse Say's Law and demand an end to profligate copying."

"If we don't do away with nuclear weapons, Say's Law will end the world the way it began—with a big bang. If the arms are available, someone will use them."

In a sense, this metaffect is proof of itself: now that it's been supplied, you'll find it everywhere you look.

The Schlepp Effect

The Yiddish word *schlepp*, derived from the German *schleppen*, means "to drag, to pull, or to carry." Perhaps because of its evocative sound, the use of the word has spread to non-Jewish populations in multiethnic cities, where it has come to signify dragging one's heels, lagging behind, delaying, or moving slowly or lazily. Schlepp has an unpleasant connotation; it suggests toil or effort. One does not schlepp to the Ritz in a limo or to the Bahamas on a cruise ship, but one does schlepp groceries in a shopping cart and schlepp one's kids to the dentist. In Los Angeles, people of all races and creeds complain about schlepping on the freeways. I got into a cab in New York not long ago and the Hispanic driver grumbled, "Oh, man, I don't want to schlepp out to the airport in this traffic."

In a 1968 *Scientific American* article titled "A Hunter's Village in Neolithic Turkey," archaeologists Dexter Perkins and Patricia Daly introduced the word *schlepp* to academia. Speculating on why certain animal parts are more prevalent at some archaeological sites than others, the husband-and-wife team suggested that in neolithic days, when hunters killed an animal far from their base camp, they carried back with them only the most useful parts—those with the most food value for the weight. If they killed a large animal fairly close to camp, the hunters might carry off the entire carcass. If they were far from camp, they would presumably butcher the animal on the spot and schlepp away only the choice cuts like the pelvis and shoulder blades, leaving behind the ribs, spine, and skull, which were not meaty enough to justify the effort. Perkins and Daly coined this hypothesis the *Schlepp Effect*.

Since its introduction, the term has also been employed by other archaeologists, principally Richard Klein of the University of Chicago, who used it to explain the relationship between location and the size of many objects, not just bones. In archaeological circles, it has therefore come to mean that the farther you are from an original source of a material, the smaller the pieces of that material you will find. Long ago in East Africa, for example, black volcanic rock was highly prized for its use in tools. Consequently, ten miles from the source of volcanic rock you now find large chunks of it; 400 miles away, you rarely find a piece larger than a half-inch thick.

British archaeologist Peter Jones attributes this to the Schlepp Effect. He theorizes that Stone-Age humans were much like their modern counterparts. If they had easy access to an ample supply of raw materials, they were quite cavalier about them. When crafting an implement, if they made a mistake, they would simply toss the rock away and pick up another chunk. When a tool began to wear thin or became dull or chipped, they might simply have discarded it. However, if they lived a great distance from the raw materials, the tribe would have conserved the stone, reusing it and resharpening it until it was the unusable little nub that archaeologists now dig up.

The Schlepp Effect can be used as a metaffect to describe certain behavior patterns. If, to save trips to the office-supply store, you buy pencils by the gross and write with them until they are smaller than your thumb; if you stock your freezer to the brim, or purchase toiletries by the ton; if, to save a trip to the city, you reschedule a luncheon date to coincide with a business meeting in the same vicinity; if you turn down an invitation to an inconvenient affair; if you pay extra for delivery services, organize car pools, order merchandise by computer, or reach out and touch someone by phone instead of in person, you are practicing a time-honored homo sapien tradition. In any epoch, no one likes to schlepp.

Metaffectively speaking, other things get whittled down the farther they get from their source. A prime example is the truth—as in the "telephone game," in which a whispered statement loses a small piece of accuracy with each transmission until, at the end of the line, it barely resembles the original. Business rumors follow the same pattern, so executives might consider this use of the metaffect: "This information has passed through a lot of hands before this report was written.

Let's confirm with the original source just in case something essential was chipped away by the Schlepp Effect."

We can schlepp emotions around as well as information, and they too can get whittled down over time. Hence, you might have a feud with an old friend and one day find yourself saying, "I think I'm ready to talk to Tom again. I've been carrying the hurt around for a long time, but the Schlepp Effect has chiseled it down to a few scraps of debris. I can't even remember what started the trouble between us."

The Stockholm Syndrome

On August 23, 1973, Jan-Erik Olssen entered the main office of Sveriges Kreditbank in Stockholm, fired a volley of shots at the ceiling with a submachine gun, and yelled in English, "The party has just begun." The party lasted six days. During that time, Olssen, a thirty-two-year-old escaped convict with a history of armed robbery, held four bank employees hostage, three young women and a man. Upon demand, Swedish officials delivered to Olssen food and a comrade (fellow convict Clark Olafsson), but they would not let him leave with the hostages.

The event dominated the Swedish media during the siege and for some time after it was resolved. But it became famous worldwide because of the mystifying reactions of the hostages: all four sided with their captors over the police. At one point, a police superintendent who was allowed to meet with the captives was astonished to find them uniformly hostile, sullen, and withdrawn, whereas they seemed convivial with their captors.

One hostage, twenty-three-year-old Kristin Ehnmark, begged Prime Minister Olaf Palme to reverse his policy and allow her and the others to leave with the robbers. She trusted them, she said; they had treated their prisoners well and would make good their promise to release them as soon as they were safe. What Ehnmark feared most was the police; she suspected they would break their word and attack, causing unnecessary carnage.

The one male hostage later said he was grateful to Olssen because the thief was going to kill him but changed his mind. At one point, Olssen promised to kill everyone including himself if the police released tear gas, because he believed exposure to the gas causes permanent brain damage. The hostages thought he was kind to make the offer.

When tear gas finally *was* used, the thieves were forced to evacuate the bank. The police demanded that the hostages be let out first. The hostages themselves refused. They were afraid that, in their absence, the cops would shoot Olssen and Olafsson. The police capitulated. When the doors opened, onlookers witnessed an amazing sight: the hostages embraced their captors and one called out, "I'll see you again."

After their ordeal, the four hostages were treated by psychiatrists, who were uniformly astonished by the friendship that had developed between captives and captors. The hostages had come to view the criminals as protectors; every simple act of consideration was viewed as an extraordinary kindness. Sometimes, in discussing decisions made by the robbers, the captives would use the word *we*. And the bond did not quickly weaken; the following year, when on vacation with her husband and children, one of the hostages obeyed a "powerful impulse" and visited Clark Olafsson in jail.

Because of this incident, the phenomenon by which captives develop sympathy for, and sometimes allegiance to, their captors has come to be called the *Stockholm Syndrome*. However, it was well-known earlier. British medical journals referred to it as "the turncoat syndrome" when it happened to prisoners of war. It was seen in German concentration camps, where some inmates fashioned swastika armbands and imitated the behavior of their Nazi captors. In airline hijackings, captive passengers frequently sympathize with the hijackers inside the cabin but not with those in the cockpit, with whom they are out of touch. One flight attendant sent gifts to a captured hijacker's prison and actually came close to marrying him. Some captives, most notably Patty Hearst, even become active collaborators.

On one level, the syndrome can be attributed to the survival instinct. When held captive, you might reason that you are less likely to be bumped off if you develop a human bond with your captors. But most experts believe that the process runs deeper than that. Brian Jenkins, an expert on terrorism for the Rand Corporation, explains it this way: a hostage is helpless; the captor is like a god. He controls when and what you eat, when you go to the bathroom, whether you live or die. At one time in life, Jenkins points out, everyone is that helpless and that dependent: when we are infants. Being a hostage, especially if you have been bound, is an infantilizing experience. Just as infants positively identify with their parents—even bad or abusive parents—so do hostages identify with their captors.

Knowing about the Stockholm Syndrome gives you more than something interesting to talk about the next time a hostage crisis dominates the news. As a metaffect, it can apply to other captivelike situations or when someone identifies strongly with a person or institution that holds the key to his or her welfare. An example is the otherwise decent human being who becomes a spokesperson for the Tobacco Institute and, as their captive, tells everyone that the carcinogenic effects of cigarettes are still unproven or not worth worrying about. Some other examples:

"I'm afraid Dave's been afflicted with the Stockholm Syndrome. Ever since he finished law school and started working for those avaricious sharks, he's lost all his idealism."

"Have you seen the way Gina dresses since she married into the Brewer family? Exactly like her mother-in-law. Hey, it's hard not to get stockholmed when you marry money."

"I've been stockholmed by my own success. I busted my butt so I could retire to a farm, but I'm such a captive to my lifestyle, I can't do without the income."

"The Stockholm Syndrome must be an occupational hazard for actors. Sara's been practically suicidal since she captured the part of Ophelia."

And, the dread of every parent: "Mom, Dad, I'm moving out before I get stockholmed into adopting all your values."

The Tomato Effect

My wife and I planted tomatoes this year. We are now eating tomatoes two or three times a day and finding new and unusual uses for them. We also cart bags of the plump red fruit to friends, who are invariably grateful. It was not always thus. Now one of America's largest commercial crops, the tomato has a checkered past.

Spanish colonists in Mexico and Peru discovered *lycopersicon esculentum* in the sixteenth century and brought it back to Europe. The delicacy soon graced tables throughout the continent, achieving mythical qualities in France, where it was known as *pomme d'amour* (love apple) and thought to be an aphrodisiac. In Italy, chefs were inspired to create magnificent sauces of *pommidoro*. Yet, despite the tomato's celebrity in the

Old World, it was shunned in the new. An eighteenth-century gardener who presented a neighbor with a bag full of round red fruit would have had the door slammed in his face. North Americans believed the tomato was poisonous.

The logic was inescapable: tomatoes belong to the nightshade family of plants, which includes belladonna and mandrake, the leaves and fruit of which can, in sufficient quantity, kill. No matter that Europeans were surviving their tomato-filled meals quite nicely, thank you. Nightshade plants were poisonous and one simply does not eat poison. And so it was not until the 1820s that North Americans began to consume tomatoes and not until this century that they were cultivated commercially.

The tomato's long march to respectability inspired two contemporary physicians to name a medical phenomenon the *Tomato Effect*. Writing in the *Journal of the American Medical Association* in May of 1984, James S. Goodwin and Jean M. Goodwin explain: "The tomato effect in medicine occurs when an efficacious treatment for a certain disease is ignored or rejected because it does not 'make sense' in the light of accepted theories of disease mechanism and drug action." In other words, just as people persisted in believing the tomato was poisonous despite ample evidence to the contrary, physicians have rejected many effective therapies because they did not make sense.

For example, from the fifth century through the Middle Ages, gout was one of the most painful and persistent afflictions in Europe. The most effective treatment for the arthritislike disorder was colchicum, an extract of the plant *Colchicum Autumnale*, which grows along the Mediterranean. But then came the Renaissance, and colchicum disappeared from the medical texts for 400 years. Its use simply did not make sense in light of the new Renaissance medical perspective, which, harking back to the classical teachings of Hippocrates and Galen, viewed all disease as the result of a general physiological imbalance rather than a singular agent like a germ or virus.

So instead of colchicum, gout was treated with bleeding and purging, generalized remedies meant to purify the system. Then, in the nineteenth century, when colchicum was found to be the active ingredient in a hugely popular patent medicine, it was reintroduced to the medical arsenal. It is still the primary treatment for acute and chronic gout.

Goodwin and Goodwin cite other examples of the Tomato Effect. At one time, the dominant theory held that rheumatoid arthritis (RA) was caused by infection. Since heavy metals were known to inhibit the growth of infection, gold salts were introduced as a treatment for RA in 1927, and by 1945 experiments had confirmed its effectiveness. However, the use of gold therapy suddenly declined. Why? Because the infection theory of rheumatoid arthritis was discredited. If RA is not an infection, medical minds reasoned, then there is no reason why gold therapy should work. Therefore, why use it? Gold returned to favor in the 1950s; since no one had yet figured out exactly what causes RA, there was no longer a valid reason to reject a treatment that works.

We have here a ripe and juicy metaffect, to be used when something useful is overlooked or rejected merely because it works in contravention to a theory that says it shouldn't. One might say that Copernicus, Darwin, and Einstein—as well as smaller fry who have been rebuked because their findings bumped heads with conventional wisdom—were temporary victims of the Tomato Effect. So was Marconi, who insisted that wireless signals could traverse the ocean even though the prevailing laws of physics "proved" they could not.

Businesses are easy prey for the Tomato Effect. Executives often get so locked into one way of doing things that offbeat approaches may as well be as poisonous as a nightshade plant. Two decades ago, U.S. automakers concluded that small, fuel-efficient cars like the ones being manufactured in Japan would never catch on in America. That was because as Detroit executives drove to work and looked out their office windows, all they saw were oversized gas guzzlers. They were tomatoed thanks to "Grosse Point Myopia," a form of conceptual near-sightedness named for the toney Detroit suburb in which many auto executives live.

Then there was the liquor company that wanted to start packaging its products in drink-sized bottles. Assuming that this would require major revamping of its production system, management hired high-priced experts to find a way to redesign the plant. Consultants were called in, handsome fees were paid, and research was conducted, but the company was unable to come up with an affordable scheme. Then an assembly-line worker came up with a solution: he drilled holes in hockey pucks, inserted the small bottles in the holes, and ran them through the existing assembly line. For seventy-five dollars, he saved that firm from the Tomato Effect.

Other applications abound. You know it's the Tomato Effect when:

Your spouse keeps returning to a pricey restaurant whose reviews are worshipful and whose reservation list overflows with VIPs—despite the fact that she complains about the food every time she eats there.

You continue to use a manual typewriter, ignoring abundant evidence that a computer will save you an enormous amount of time.

An ethnocentric friend keeps taking painkillers for back spasms even though you cured an identical problem with acupuncture, because he believes that if you use anything Chinese you'll have to do it again an hour later.

You keep following your brother's financial advice instead of your wife's, because he is a CPA and your wife's conclusions spring solely from intuition—even though she's right more often than your brother.

You've been a track coach for thirty years and you still teach high-jumpers the straddle jump, because there's no rational reason why the Fosbury Flop should work (see page 93).

In short, knowing about the Tomato Effect can be a deterrent to rigid thinking. If something appears useful, even if you think it can't be, give it a taste. New ideas are not necessarily poisonous.

The Twins Effect

Your high school reunion is coming up and you can't wait to see your old friend Charlie. You and he were like brothers. You did everything together—you even dated sisters. Then, at the reunion, your dreams of rekindling a glorious friendship are shattered; you and Charlie have nothing in common. It's as if you've been on different planets all these years. Metaffectively, you've just experienced the *Twins Effect*, one of the more startling consequences of Einstein's theory of relativity.

Prior to the Einsteinian revolution, it was believed that time and space were absolute and universal, always the same for everyone everywhere. To most of us, that is still the way it is (or ought to be). But Einstein demonstrated that time is elastic; it can be stretched and squeezed like a rubber band. In fact, each of us carries around his or her own personal timepiece, which is different from the next person's. If Archie moves while Jeanette remains stationary, less time passes for Archie than for Jeanette. This is known as time dilation, and it is not just a theoretical knickknack; it is very real.

We don't notice time dilation in everyday life because we

move about too slowly for its effect to register. If you are on a train whizzing by a station, the clock on the platform will run slightly slower for you than for someone standing on the platform, although that distortion is far too small to be detected by the naked eye. However, thanks to extraordinarily sensitive instruments, physicists have been observing and measuring time-dilation phenomena since Einstein's day.

The Twins Effect, also known as the Twins Paradox, is the most famous of the relativistic mind-bogglers. Say one twin blasts off in a spaceship, soars to a nearby star at four-fifths the speed of light, and returns to earth ten years later. At the reunion, the twin who remained on earth will be ten years older than he was when they last met; the traveling twin will be only six years older. Like Dorian Gray and his portrait, they will have aged at different rates. If the astronaut twin were to travel at a speed even closer to that of light (186,000 miles per second), he might age only a year to his brother's ten.

Psychologically, the Twins Effect is all around us. As time passes, some of us speed through life while others meander, and most of us find ourselves becoming vastly different from friends, siblings, and lovers with whom we once felt a certain twinship: "I ran into my old roommate today. It was positively Einsteinian. Back then we were inseparable, but now we're light-years apart. I guess it's just a case of the Twins Effect."

Our inner selves can get confounded by a kind of Twins Effect too. For example, think of those on the fast track who find themselves lamenting that the old, fun-loving part of themselves was left far behind. Perhaps they've been victimized by an intrapsychic Twins Effect. Their internal twins have a lot of catching up to do.

Suppose, at age fifty-five, you gear all your finances and business affairs toward retirement at sixty-five. The decade passes and the last thing you feel like doing is retiring. Call your accountant, your business associates, your lawyer, and your family, and tell them you've changed your mind due to the Twins Effect—you aged differently from the way you'd expected: "I must have been in some other orbit the past ten years. Let's just say my evil twin signed these documents."

Perhaps the metaffect can even apply to material objects. When two people buy the same make and model car, and five years later one car looks as good as new while the other is ready for the junk heap, call it the Twins Effect.

In his book *God and the New Physics*, Paul Davies writes, "In a sense, we are all travellers in time, heading toward the future, but the elasticity of time enables some people to get there faster than others. Rapid motion enables you to put the brakes on your own time scale, and let the world rush by, as it were." Davies meant it quite literally, but the metaffective implications of the statement are profound.

Consider those people who rush helter-skelter through life, the sort of folks who pride themselves in never wasting a second, whose motto seems to be "time is money" and who express their personal philosophies in clichés like "live hard, play hard." To them, the rest of humanity seem like plodders, tortoises in a race only hares can win. If you are one of those speedsters, you can argue that the Twins Effect gives you the racer's edge; the twin who hurtles through space ages less than his stationary brother.

However, if you are among the slowpokes, you can contend that the metaffect should not be taken that literally. Tell your flying friend, "You think the Twins Effect will keep you young, but if you don't take some time out for silence and stillness, the world will rush past you before you can learn anything. You may think I'm killing time, but in fact, time is killing you."

The Wallenda Factor

In 1978 the world's premiere aerialist, Karl Wallenda, set foot on a tightrope in San Juan, Puerto Rico. In most respects the performance was like all the others in his storied career. But there was one crucial exception: Wallenda's attitude. "All Karl thought about for three straight months prior to it was *falling*," said his wife. "It was the first time he'd ever thought about that, and it seemed to me that he put all his energies into *not falling* rather than walking the tightrope."

Wallenda, who had always seemed impervious to danger, was suddenly obsessed with the possibility that he might fall. For the first time, he personally supervised the installation of the rope and checked to see that the guy wires were secure. Despite his preoccupation, or perhaps because of it, he fell seventy-five feet to his death.

Based upon Mrs. Wallenda's account of her husband's death, management expert Warren Bennis recognized an important metaffect for those in leadership positions. In all his interviews with high-ranking executives, he had never heard one use the word *failure*. They instead used terms such as *mistake, glitch, mess, error*, or *setback*, perhaps because the "F" word has a sense of finality about it whereas the others imply only a temporary condition. In his book *Leaders*, Bennis writes that successful people are not intimidated by setbacks; they learn from them and use them as springboards to action. By way of illustration, he quotes an anonymous executive who said, "A mistake is just another way of doing things."

In other words, Bennis felt that successful people approach tasks the way Karl Wallenda did until his fatal slip: they hop on the wire and start walking, eyes on the goal, uninhibited by the thought of failure. That attitude he dubbed the *Wallenda Factor*, choosing to emphasize Karl Wallenda's record of fearless success rather than the single exception that proved the rule. Bennis defines the factor as "the capacity to embrace positive goals, to pour one's energies into the task, not into looking behind and dredging up excuses for past events."

The implication is clear: if you approach a task thinking about *not* failing, or *not* embarrassing yourself, or *not* losing money or face or whatever, you run the risk of creating a self-fulfilling prophecy in which your worst nightmare comes true. You certainly would not make an inspiring leader. Imagine, for example, an athletic coach leading his charges onto the playing field with the inspiring words, "Let's go out there and not make fools of ourselves."

Bennis uses two basketball legends to illustrate the point. John Wooden, the "Wizard of Westwood," who led UCLA to ten national championships in twelve years, once said, "Failure is not the crime. Low aim is." And Ray Meyer, who led DePaul University to forty-two consecutive winning seasons, said when asked how he felt after a winning streak was stopped, "Great! Now we can start concentrating on winning, not on not losing."

Successful people, says Warren Bennis, possess the Wallenda Factor. They have the capacity to embrace positive goals, to zero in on a task and take control without worrying about the possibility of failure; if a setback occurs, they find a way to use it to their advantage.

But the Wallenda Factor is not just for leaders and executives. It applies to many areas of life:

When you're so concerned about not soiling your brand-new fifty-dollar necktie that you spill ketchup on your five-hundred-dollar suit, you've forgotten the Wallenda Factor.

When you find yourself trembling as the hour of your public speech draws near, remember Karl Wallenda. You might be thinking about *not* sounding like an idiot instead of how you're going to dazzle your audience.

When your child is facing a major exam and she's so sure she's going to fail that she can neither sleep nor concentrate on her studies, wallenda her with a pep talk that turns her thoughts away from the fear of failing.

When your associates are so obsessed with the possibility of not succeeding that they start to act tentatively and cautiously, tell them, "What this outfit needs is the Wallenda Factor. Anyone who cares more about not screwing up than he does about performing with excellence should go join the clowns. We want high-wire acts around here."

The Werther Effect

In 1774, twenty-eight-year-old Johann Wolfgang von Goethe first attracted the public acclaim that would ultimately make him one of the world's most renowned literary figures. A great poet, dramatist, novelist, and even scientist, Goethe that year published *The Sorrows of Young Werther,* an epistolary novel about a young man who kills himself. Goethe wrote the book largely for therapeutic reasons— like his titular hero, he had been severely depressed over an unrequited love—and the work enabled him to achieve a catharsis of sorts.

For the reading public, however, the novel's effect was tragic. A huge popular success in Goethe's native Germany and in other European countries, the book prompted so many young men to imitate Werther's suicide—even dressed in the same style of waistcoat that the character wore—that authorities banned it.

In 1974 David Phillips, a sociologist at the University of California at San Diego, drew upon that bit of literary history in coining the term *Werther Effect* (pronounced *vair*-tuh). One of many social scientists now studying the role of imitation in deviant behavior, Dr. Phillips set out to see whether well-publicized suicides spark an increase in suicides in the general population.

For his first study, Phillips gathered a systematic list of all the suicide stories that appeared on the front page of the *New York Times* over a twenty-year period. He then analyzed government records to see if the number of suicides committed in the week following the publicized suicides was greater than the normal rate for that time frame. The number turned out to be significantly higher after twenty-six of the thirty-three stories; hence, the Werther Effect.

Phillips went on to use more sophisticated statistical procedures and always he found the same result. In one study, he analyzed the daily fluctuations of more than 12,000 teenage suicides between 1973 and 1979. It turned out that when the television networks carried a suicide story, the rate of teen suicides increased significantly the subsequent week. The rate fell back to normal following that period. Furthermore, the more publicity the story attracted, the greater the increase in suicides the following week.

Can we be certain that the increase in suicides was due to imitative behavior? Phillips himself is sanguine about the conclusion. He analyzed several alternative explanations (such as that prior conditions precipitated a wave of suicides of which the publicized cases were only examples), and he found compelling statistical reasons to reject each one. Phillips' studies also confirmed two common perceptions: teenagers are more likely than adults to mimic, and teenage girls are more imitative than boys.

Social scientists have found a kind of Werther Effect in areas other than suicide. In lab studies, for example, subjects shown

a violent film are more likely to exhibit aggressive behavior than those who view, say, "Mister Rogers" or a documentary on birds. Phillips also says that media stories about violence precipitate an increase in violent acts, especially if the publicized violence is rewarding and exciting. For example, he found a statistical correlation between heavyweight-championship fights—well-publicized, socially sanctioned, highly rewarded acts of violence—and violent behavior among the public. (In the same study, he found another distressing bit of data: when the loser of the match was white, the number of violent crimes involving white victims increased significantly more than incidents with black victims; when the loser of the fight was black, the opposite occurred. This is called victim modeling.)

In short, the Werther Effect is about the imitation of highly publicized destructive behavior. Metaffectively, though, it can be extended to the imitation of *any* attention-getting behavior, and we needn't look too far for examples of wertherization. Consider the impact of popular culture. Clark Gable dealt a crushing blow to the undershirt business when he removed his shirt in *It Happened One Night* to reveal a bare chest. It's a good bet that thousands of men tripped themselves, not the light fantastic, in clumsy attempts to imitate Fred Astaire, and many more may have shortened their life spans by smoking in the Bogey manner in hopes of appealing to a slinky Lauren Bacall–type babe.

Many a cross-country car trip was inspired by Jack Kerouac's *On the Road*. The nihilism remained intact a generation later, but the route, the favored intoxicants, and the mode of transport were changed by *Easy Rider*. In the fifties young men groomed themselves like Elvis, in the sixties like the Beatles. After *Flashdance*, teenage girls wore oversized, strategically torn, off-the-shoulder sweatshirts; then they flip-flopped the foundations of fashion by wearing lacy undergarments on the outside à la Madonna. Can the wave of yuppie pregnancies in the late eighties be attributed to the fertility of the couples on "thirtysomething"? Has the resurgence of monogamy been abetted by *Fatal Attraction*? What sort of Werther Effects will the nineties bring?

Advertisers and promoters today are so skilled at stimulating imitative behavior that we have to be eternally vigilant lest we find ourselves inadvertently falling into step. At the rate MTV is going, we might all soon be wearing pulled-back hair and tight black skirts or one-day stubble and a single earring.

Returning to the more serious issues from which the metaffect was drawn, some Los Angeles police believe that the rash of freeway snipers that hit that city in 1989 was inspired by the publicity garnered by the initial incidents. Many experts feel that hostage-takers have been encouraged, at least in part, by the notoriety achieved by their early role models. Imitation is widely assumed to be instrumental in teenage drug abuse. If your teens are bored by bromides like "Just say no!" and the words "peer pressure" are as grating to their ears as Twisted Sister is to yours, you might try to educate them with this metaffect: "I know you're too smart and too independent to get swept up in some silly Werther Effect."

Then again, the Werther Effect can have its virtues. When celebrities are shown working for a worthwhile cause, it appears to inspire socially responsible behavior among their admirers. When a public figure loses weight, it seems that thousands decide to do the same. When a prominent personality undergoes treatment for substance abuse, chances are enrollment increases at clinics around the country.

Perhaps it's time to make positive use of the Werther Effect. For example, think of the environmental impact it might create if macho television cops start arresting people for littering or wasting water.

The Zeigarnik Effect

Do you find it difficult to stop thinking about your work? If thoughts of an unfinished project plague you at supper, intrude on your leisure, or wake you up at night, you are experiencing in real life what in psychological research is called the *Zeigarnik Effect*.

The term was named for a Russian scientist named Bluma Zeigarnik. As a student in Berlin, Zeigarnik worked with the influential American psychologist Kurt Lewin, who postulated that tension is created whenever an individual develops a psychological need or establishes a goal. Under those conditions, a force acts upon the person, propelling him or her to behave so as to fulfill the goal and to *think* about the associated activity even when not performing it. Only when the goal or need is met is the tension released.

Based on Lewin's theories, Zeigarnik reasoned that if a goal-oriented activity is interrupted, the person will remember the task better than he will recall projects that were completed. The tension related to the incomplete tasks will persist, thereby strengthening the memory.

In 1927, Zeigarnik designed a study to test that hypothesis. She gave 138 children a number of tasks involving mental arithmetic, puzzle solving, clay modeling, and other activities. Half of the assignments were interrupted, while the other half were carried through to completion. An hour later, the children were asked to name the tasks they had been given. One hundred and ten had better recall of the interrupted tasks than the completed ones; only seventeen remembered the completed tasks better, and eleven remembered both equally well.

Zeigarnik and other researchers subsequently expanded and refined her initial findings. It was found that the stronger the motivation associated with the interrupted activity and the closer it is to completion when interrupted, the stronger the Zeigarnik Effect will be; in other words, a greater percentage of uncompleted tasks will be remembered. For example, if you are writing a passionate love letter and are suddenly called to a meeting just before you express your deepest feelings, it's a sure bet that when you return you will remember what you still need to write but not a word of what you've already written.

Subjective evaluations also alter the effect. When subjects were told they had been working quite successfully before their tasks were interrupted, they tended to forget them, just as they did the finished tasks. The feeling of success evidently can serve the same tension-reducing function as completing the activity. Interestingly, the Zeigarnik Effect can be reversed if the person believes that not finishing the task is a personal failure; when self-esteem is on the line, we tend to remember our successes and forget our failures.

Now you know what to say when your spouse can't stop phoning the office on your vacation or takes along a briefcase full of work when you visit your parents for the weekend: "Don't mind him, it's just that damned Zeigarnik Effect. He couldn't finish his work before we left and now he can't forget about it." If such behavior goes too far, you can use the metaffect to reverse it: "Honey, come to bed. I know the report was due on Friday, but you don't want to zeigarnik our sex life, do you?"

The metaffective potential expands if you think of the word *incomplete* in psychological terms. For instance, you probably have at least one long-gone relationship that persists in your memory, one you recall more frequently and with greater clarity of detail than relationships that actually lasted longer. Perhaps important feelings remain unexpressed; perhaps emotional connections were never made, secrets never revealed, experiences never shared, promises never kept, or desires never fulfilled. Perhaps you had an unrequited love; due to its incompleteness, it intrudes on the present more vividly than affairs that ran their course: "You know, it's funny. There was this guy I met on a spring break once. We kind of lost each other before the week was up, and I never saw him again. Yet I think about him far more often than my ex-boyfriend. He must have zeigarniked me."

Implicit in this metaffect is some practical advice. If you want to get away from it all, before you leave the office, clear your desk (or at least your mind); clarify all ambiguous discussions; resolve all arguments and tidy up all the loose ends. And in your personal life, find an acceptable way to express your negative feelings so you don't get zeigarniked into carrying them around with you.

The metaffect might also serve as a useful warning signal. If you find yourself thinking about something persistently, if you can't get it out of your mind, you might take it as a clue that something about it remains imcomplete. "Bring that report back in here, please. I have to review that data before it's submitted. I'm having a strong Zeigarnik Effect."

Or, "Hello, Jill? This is Jack. . . . No, actually it's been *three* years. . . . To what do you owe the honor? Well, to the Zeigarnik Effect, actually. See, I can't stop thinking about you. We must have left something unresolved."

Afterword

Do you know any metaffects? Are there any principles, laws, or syndromes in your line of work whose definitions are interesting and rich enough to be used metaphorically? How about your hobby? Your favorite sport? Have you come across any in a book or magazine? Have you or your friends or members of your family invented any terms with the potential to become metaffects?

If so, you can contribute to the next collection by sending us your suggestions. Define the terms and tell us their origins and how you think they can be used metaphorically. Of course, we can't guarantee that your contribution will find its way into the volume, nor can we offer any compensation other than a promise to credit you by name if your metaffect is used (assuming it is you who first brings it to our attention).

Send your suggestions to Metaffects, Jeremy P. Tarcher, Inc., 5858 Wilshire Boulevard, Los Angeles, California 90036.